Featherstone

fantastic ideas for
investigations

PHILL AND SALLY FEATHERSTONE

Featherstone
An imprint of Bloomsbury Publishing Plc

50 Bedford Square
London
WC1B 3DP
UK

1385 Broadway
New York
NY 10018
USA

www.bloomsbury.com

Bloomsbury is a registered trademark of Bloomsbury Publishing Plc

First published 2016

British Library Cataloguing-in-Publication Data
A catalogue record for this book is available from the British Library.

ISBN:
PB 978-1-4729-1916-8
ePDF 978-1-4729-1917-5

Library of Congress Cataloging-in-Publication Data
A catalogue record for this book is available from the Library of Congress.

1 3 5 7 9 10 8 6 4 2

Printed and bound in India by Replika Pvt Ltd.

This book is produced using paper that is made from wood grown in managed, sustainable
forests. It is natural, renewable and recyclable. The logging and manufacturing processes
conform to the environmental regulations of the country of origin.

To view more of our titles please visit www.bloomsbury.com

Acknowledgements
With special thanks to Academia Cuscatleca, British School, San Salvador;
Sam Goodman; Sue Gascoigne who supported us with such fabulous photographs.

Contents

Introduction

Investigation is part of the early years curriculum for science, and appears in statements such as this description of Understanding the World:

> '**Understanding the world** involves guiding children to make sense of their physical world and their community through opportunities to explore, observe and find out about people, places, technology and the environment.'

Statutory Framework for the Early Years FoundationStage DfE 2012

By the time children leave the Early Years Foundation Stage (EYFS) they should be able to fulfill the criteria in the relevant Early Learning Goal:

> '**The world:** children know about similarities and differences in relation to places, objects, materials and living things. They talk about the features of their own immediate environment and how environments might vary from one another. They make observations of animals and plants and explain why some things occur, and talk about changes.'

Statutory Framework for the EYFS; DfE; 2012

However, there is another strand that runs throughout the latest guidance for the EYFS. The Characteristics of Effective Learning are indicators that the process of learning is an active and permanent part of children's experiences in early years settings. These characteristics are the 'how' of learning, underpinning and enriching the 'what' of learning. The Characteristics are described in this way:

> 'In planning and guiding children's activities, practitioners must reflect on the different ways that children learn and reflect these in their practice. Three characteristics of effective teaching and learning are:
>
> * **playing and exploring** – children investigate and experience things, and 'have a go';
>
> * **active learning** – children concentrate and keep on trying if they encounter difficulties, and enjoy achievements; and
>
> * **creating and thinking critically** – children have and develop their own ideas, make links between ideas, and develop strategies for doing things.'

Statutory Framework for the EYFS; DfE; 2012

These key statements are at the heart of 50 Fantastic Ideas for Investigations, and we hope the book will help practitioners and their managers to offer early experiences of science through interesting and active investigations.

The role of the practitioner

Practitioners are an essential part of effective learning, and throughout the book, we have attempted to encourage practitioners to use the principles of sustained shared thinking – an activity in which 'Two or more individuals 'work together' in an intellectual way to solve a problem, clarify a concept, evaluate an activity, extend a narrative etc.'

This involves the adult in engaging in activities that, while they are planned, are also open-ended, leaving the children plenty of space to comment, investigate and experiment, and to affect the course of the exploration. The adult role in these activities is a sensitive one, and involves:

* open questioning

* open ended resources

* watching and listening

* giving support while knowing when to stand back

* knowing that observation is at the heart of accurate assessment

* understanding that 'process' is more important and valuable than a simple 'product'.

We understand how difficult this is, particularly at a time when evidence is required for every judgement, and outcomes are often measured by paper, not process.

Every activity follows the same format, but in the interests of practitioner confidence, and the expectations of many managers, we have included some additional support and guidance within each activity:

1. The activities require simple, everyday resources and equipment, most of it available in every setting. Some activities need additional resources but we have tried to keep these as affordable as possible, given the current financial restrictions in most settings. Magnifying glasses, bug catchers and capacity measures are the only essential scientific equipment to complete all 50 investigations.

2. Every activity has a clear science focus, which is identified on the page, and encourages the use of scientific language and terminology. We have used 'official' scientific language to describe the central focus, as it is important to link the EYFS language with that of the National Curriculum, partly in the interests of continuity, and partly so practitioners and their managers can be confident that such investigations are forming a real foundation for work in later years.

3. On every page you will find 'Fascinating facts', which are either relevant to the activity, or which include simple scientific information to help practitioners answer children's questions. You can find lots of additional information on the internet.

4. We have included a photographer in the list of essentials at the beginning of the list of 'What you need', to remind practitioners that photographic evidence is the most powerful evidence of their professionalism and of children's achievements. If you don't have access to an early years digital camera, we suggest that practitioners might use their mobile phones. We realise that schools and settings take advantage of this facility, but also realise that budgets often don't stretch to cameras for children to use. If you do have a school/setting camera, you can make the job of photographer more important by making or finding a special photographer's hat, jacket, high visibility waistcoat or even a lanyard with a photographer's special pass.

5. Each activity includes a range of suggested open questions to ask the children during the exploration. These questions are in italics, and are intended to keep the focus clearly on scientific exploration, as it can be tempting to 'wander off target' and turn the activity into messy play, art and design, or mathematics. You don't have to ask them all! The sample questions are just that: examples of the sort of questions that keep the children's focus (and yours) on the science, and to get you started. Of course practitioners will think of more, and others will arise once you begin an exploration.

6. Of course, literacy is the cornerstone of all learning, and specific vocabulary is a part of learning about science. At the end of this introduction, we have included a vocabulary list, complete with meanings. This list is not a complete scientific vocabulary, just some of the words you could include with these particular investigations.

As you begin to use the ideas in the book, we hope the activities will spark off other ideas for things to investigate and more questions to ask about the world and the many fascinating things it contains. You can expand your horizons to explorations in your garden, the park, the local shopping centre, or even on walks, visits and more formal expeditions. A few magnifying glasses, bug catchers, and a camera can turn the simplest walk into a scientific investigation, where you can see children's thinking expanding, and know you are really doing the job of an early years practitioner – joining children in their learning and helping them to become scientists for life.

Know your oats

Investigate a box of porridge

What you need:

- A camera
- A clipboard
- A bag or box of porridge oats
- A picture of oats growing
- A tray or shallow box
- Scales or balance
- Magnifying glasses, spoons, water in a jug or plastic bottle
- Saucepan and wooden spoon
- Small bowls or yogurt pots and spoons
- Honey, milk
- Access to a stove or microwave

Top tip

Showing the children a transparent bag of oats will make the first stages of this investigation easier.

Taking it forward

- Use dry or wet porridge oats in your sand tray instead of sand, or investigate other sorts of breakfast cereals.

What's in it for the children?

Scientific processes: Materials, changes through heating.

Fascinating fact: Oat grains are flattened between rollers to break the hard shell of the seed.

✚ Health & Safety

Check for any allergies or intolerances, and if necessary buy 'free-from' products. Take care with hot surfaces and objects.

What to do:

1. Help the children to collect all the things you need. Appoint a photographer, and make sure they know what they can do (move around, choose what to photograph etc.)

2. Sit together and pass the packet of oats around, talking about what you can see, what is in the packet, and if the children know what it is.

3. Look at any pictures and help them to read the information on the pack – including the weight (which you can check with your scales), the ingredients, and the instructions for cooking. Talk about what oats are and how they grow. Look at the pictures of oats growing. *Does the porridge in the pack look different from growing grains of oats? What has happened to them?*

4. Tip some of the oats (not the whole pack) into a tray or a small bowl and let the children investigate it with fingers, magnifying glasses and spoons. Smell and taste the raw oats. Talk about why it feels and looks the way it does.

5. Add some cold water to the oats and talk about what happens. *Why doesn't the mixture look like porridge? What else must we do to turn it into porridge?* Take some photos.

6. Look at the pack again and read any instructions about making porridge. *Can you find the answer?* Discuss the instructions and use them to make porridge together with the rest of the oats from the pack. Use a saucepan on a stove or a plastic bowl in a microwave!

7. Look at the cooked porridge. *What has changed? Can you smell or feel any difference in the cooked porridge?*

8. Tip the porridge into pots or bowls and add milk and a little honey to each. Taste the porridge together as you tell the story of 'Goldilocks and the Three Bears'.

Wibble wobble

Investigate a block of jelly

What you need:

- A camera
- A clipboard
- **Several blocks of jelly of different colours** (not jelly powder or crystals)
- **Plastic bowls** (transparent if possible)
- Spoons
- **Magnifying glasses, water in a jug or plastic bottle, measuring jug**
- **A kettle** (adult only)
- **Jelly moulds or small containers**
- **Small fruit such as blueberries, cherries, grapes or raspberries** (optional)

Top tip ⭐

Clean, new sand moulds, or silicone cake cases make good jelly moulds.

Taking it forward

- Make some more jellies with powdered or leaf gelatine and fruit juice, and talk about the difference.

What's in it for the children?

Scientific processes: Changes - Melting, dissolving and setting.

Fascinating fact: Animal gelatine is made from bones of animals, vegetable gelatine is made from carrageen, a sort of seaweed, or from a sort of moss.

➕ Health & Safety

Sugar free jellies are healthier. Take care with the hot water and be aware of any children who might not eat jelly for vegetarian reasons.

What to do:

1. Help the children to collect all the things you need. Appoint a photographer.

2. Sit together and ask the children if they know how to make jelly, and what jelly is made from. Pass the packets of jelly around. Feel the jelly block, and talk about the weight, colours and wobbly texture of the jelly inside. *What is it?*

3. *Do you know how to make jelly from this stuff? What do you think we need to do?* If no one knows how to make jelly, ask them how they think they can make this packet into a jelly to eat. Listen carefully to their ideas, and be prepared to try them out.

4. Cut or tear one of the jelly blocks into pieces and try different ideas with each piece: putting cold water with one, putting one in the microwave, putting one in the sun. Try anything the children suggest, even though it might seem odd to you! Take photos of each experiment.

5. Look at the wrappers to see if there are any instructions, and try these alongside, not instead of, the children's ideas, so you can compare results. Take care with the hot water, and use just enough to melt the jelly, then top it up with cold water. This will make the jelly set faster, as well as being safer. Talk about what happens as the jelly melts, and look at it with magnifying glasses.

6. When the jellies are mixed, even the ones that don't seem to be working, pour them into the jelly moulds and add some fruit if you like.

7. Put these jellies somewhere cool to set.

8. Check on the jellies once in a while to see what is happening as they set. *Why are some of them setting more quickly? Why are some not setting at all? Why have some bits of jelly not even melted?*

9. Try your jellies with small spoons. *Which experiments worked best?*

Pasta all sorts

Investigate a packet of pasta shapes

What you need:

- A camera
- A clipboard
- A big bag of dry pasta shapes – 'alphabetti' shapes are great for this activity, but a couple of packs of other shapes would work well too
- A tray or shallow box
- Small bowls or yogurt pots, small spoons
- Magnifying glasses, spoons, water in a jug or plastic bottle
- Saucepan and wooden spoon
- Some grated cheese
- Access to a stove

Top tip

Transparent bags of pasta will make the first stages of the investigation easier.

Taking it forward

- Try making your own pasta – look for a recipe on the internet – and make your own shapes and designs.

What's in it for the children?

Scientific processes: Materials, changes through heating.

Fascinating fact: Pasta is usually made from durum, a sort of wheat flour.

Health & Safety

Check for any allergies or intolerances, and if necessary buy 'free-from' products.

What to do:

1. Help the children to collect all the things you need. Appoint a photographer.

2. Sit together and pass the packets of pasta around, talking about what you can see, what is in the packets, and if the children know what it is.

3. Ask what pasta is made from, and see if you can find out from the packet. *Is there anything else in the pasta? Why is pasta different from the flour you use for cooking, or from porridge oats? How does it get so hard and in shapes? Could we make some pasta ourselves?* Listen to their ideas and take them all seriously.

4. Tip some of the dry pasta into a tray or box and let the children feel it. *Do you know the names of the different shapes (spirals, macaroni, etc)?* Talk about the texture and smell of the pasta. *Why is it hard? Could you eat it now?* Let them try if they want to. *How does pasta get soft enough to eat?* Let them try adding water or other liquids to small quantities of pasta in bowls. *Can we find out how to cook pasta from the packet?*

5. Now tip some the pasta into the tray and give the children some small pots for a sorting and classifying challenge – collecting similar shapes, making patterns or words, separate the spirals from the macaroni etc.

6. Now cook some of the pasta and when it is cool let the children play with it in an empty water tray. Remind them not to eat this pasta as they have played with it.

7. You could cook some more pasta for the children to eat, and sprinkle it with grated cheese.

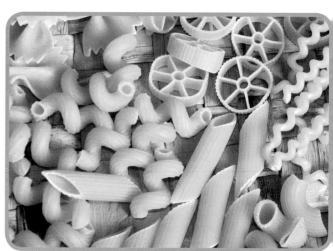

Soft structures

Investigate a bag of small marshmallows

What you need:

- A camera
- A clipboard
- **A big bag of small marshmallows** (the sort for putting in hot drinks)
- **A packet of cocktail sticks** (or dry spaghetti if you are worried about safety)
- **Safe plastic knives**
- **Small plastic trays or boards** (children's pastry boards would be ideal)
- **Milk and chocolate drink powder**
- **Access to microwave or stove** (optional).

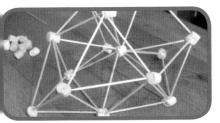

Taking it forward

- Make some more structures with sticks and clay or soaked dried chickpeas or peas and cocktail sticks.

What's in it for the children?

Scientific processes: Materials and their properties, structures.

Fascinating fact: Marshmallows are made from whipped sugar, and coated with corn flour.

✚ Health & Safety

Teach children to use cocktail sticks with care. Be aware of children who might not eat marshmallows because they are vegetarian.

What to do:

1. Help the children to collect all the things you need. Appoint a photographer.

2. Sit together and talk first about the marshmallows. Offer the bag to each child so the can take one to eat if they want to. *What does marshmallow taste like? How does it feel in your mouth?*

3. Explain that the rest of the marshmallows are for a science experiment and children will be handling them, so they will not be good to eat. Tip a few marshmallows on each tray or board, and concentrate on the texture and appearance of the marshmallows, not their taste or smell, although both of these will be tempting!

4. Try cutting some in half to see what is inside. *What makes them so squishy and soft? Can you see anything special that might make them soft and sticky inside, but not sticky on the outside? How do you think marshmallows are made? Can we find out from the packet? Can we find out from the internet or books?*

5. Now tip some of the cocktail sticks onto the trays and talk about the differences between the sticks and the marshmallows. Encourage descriptive words such as: soft, hard, stiff, dry, springy, spongy, powdery, pointy, etc. Emphasise safety with sticks.

6. Investigate how you could fix the marshmallows together using the spaghetti or cocktail sticks to make structures. *Can you make a triangle shape? A square? A cube? Can we make a structure that will stand up on its own? Can we join two structures to make a bigger one?*

7. Give the children time to explore these materials. Don't forget to encourage your photographer to take plenty of photos!

8. At the end of the investigation, make some warm chocolate milk drinks and melt some fresh marshmallows in them. Watch what happens to the marshmallows in the hot milk.

Top tip ⭐

Don't put all the marshmallows out at once, save some for later and for drinks.

Look at you!

Investigate hair

What you need:

- A camera
- A clipboard
- A recent, full-face photo of every child in the group. This is a useful resource for a lot of different activities – they'll last longer if you laminate them
- Chalk, a big piece of paper and markers for the block graphs

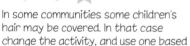

Top tip ⭐

In some communities some children's hair may be covered. In that case change the activity, and use one based on size of hands or feet instead.

What to do:

1. Collect all the things you need and appoint a photographer, but make sure they are included in this activity.

2. Sit in a circle on the floor. Ask the children: *Who is the tallest in the group? Who is the shortest?* Remain sensitive to any personal observations the children make and discourage any insensitive or inappropriate remarks particularly regarding skin colour or race.

3. Ask the tallest child and the shortest child to stand at opposite sides of the circle. Then ask all the other children to stand up and arrange themselves in order of height between the tallest and shortest children, changing places as they organise themselves – the photographer could help to check this. When they're happy it's right, record the actual order in a photo.

4. Now sit down again, and ask the children to cover their eyes. Without looking, ask them to say what is the most common hair colour in the group, then open their eyes and look.

5. Try again. *Guess the most common eye colour? Do more people have curly hair than straight? Do more people have long hair than short?* Let them open their eyes to check each one. Record their answers.

6. Spread out the children's photographs and draw three circles on the floor with chalk (or make circles with skipping ropes). Label the circles 'black', 'brown', 'fair or blonde'.

7. Ask each child to put his or her own photo in the right circle. You will probably have some discussions here, and may have to add another circle!

8. When everyone has placed his/her own photo, wait for the photographer to take a photograph. Count how many photos are in each circle. *Were their estimates/guesses right?* Then each child retrieves her/his own photo.

9. Remove the circles, and ask the children if they know how to sort the information about hair colour in a different way. Try any suggestions.

10. Draw a line on the floor, and put the hair colour labels in a row under the line. Ask each child to place his/her photo above the line, making a column of photos, to make a photographic block graph. Tell the children this is a block graph, and ask them if they think this way or the circles is the best way to organise information.

Taking it forward

- After the height exercise, ask the children to say whether they think the height order they've recorded will be the same in Year 1. You won't be able to test this, yet, but it makes for an interesting discussion.

What's in it for the children?

Scientific processes: Human body, similarities and differences, classification and grouping.

Fascinating fact: Your hair colour comes from your genes, through your parents and depends on the amount of melanin in your hair. The more melanin your hair has, the darker its colour.

Cool it!

Investigate a bunch of bananas

What you need:

- A camera
- A clipboard
- A bunch or bag of bananas (one for every two or three children)
- Safe plastic knives and forks
- **Boards** (white boards or pastry boards would be ideal)
- **A piece of fabric, such as a tea towel**
- Scales or balance
- **Magnifying glasses**
- **Small bowls or yogurt pots and spoons**
- Access to a freezer

Top tip

Try to get varying sizes of bananas.

Taking it forward

- Freeze other small fruits such as blueberries or raspberries, and make sugar-free frozen snack with these too.

What's in it for the children?

Scientific processes: Sorting and classifying; changes through freezing.

Fascinating fact: Freezing breaks down the cell walls and makes the banana creamy.

Health & Safety

This activity needs clean hands. Be aware of any food allergies or intolerances.

What to do:

1. Wash your hands and help the children to collect all the things you need. Appoint a photographer, and make sure they know they can join in.

2. Sit together and pass the bananas around, without peeling them. See how many words you can find to describe the bananas: their texture, colour, smell.

3. Help them to put the bananas in order of length on the cloth or tea towel. Use words such as long, longer, longest, shortest, fattest, thinnest to describe the different bananas. *Is the longest banana also the heaviest? What do you think?* Record their guesses on your clipboard.

4. Use the scales to check and re-order the bananas by weight, and talk about the differences. *Were our guesses right?*

5. Now let the children work together to peel the bananas and cut them into halves or thirds so everyone has a piece of their own.

6. Gently investigate the bananas with your eyes and other senses, and use magnifying glasses too. *Look at the insides, what can you see?*

7. Using safe knives help them to cut the bananas into slices. Don't worry about even slices. *Do you think we could make these bananas into ice cream? How could we do it?*

8. Pile the slices in plastic bowls or even in small plastic bags, and freeze until solid.

9. Take the frozen bananas out of the freezer, and while they are still frozen, use a fork to mash them well and they will turn into banana ice-cream! Eat and enjoy, talking about how the banana has changed in the cold freezer. *How did the bananas turn into ice cream?*

My spud, your spud

What you need:

- A camera
- A clipboard
- A bag of washed potatoes, enough for one each and a few spares
- Boards: pastry boards or whiteboards
- Magnifying glasses, spoons
- Safe plastic knives, adult vegetable knives (for the adults!)
- Water, milk, potato masher, a little butter (optional)
- A big bowl or saucepan and access to a cooker or microwave

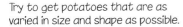

Top tip ⭐

Try to get potatoes that are as varied in size and shape as possible.

Health & Safety

Raw potato tastes nasty, but warn the children not to eat it anyway.

What to do:

1. Help the children to collect all the things you need. Appoint a photographer.

2. Sit together and pass the bag of potatoes round so every child can pick one. Talk about where potatoes come from. *What do they turn into when we cook them?*

3. Give the children some time to look carefully at their own potato, every one will be different, but they may not have realised this yet. Now let them use 'Talk partners' in pairs to tell their neighbour about their potato, using describing words.

4. Take turns to say 'My potato is…'. Remind the children that you are trying to find as many different words as you can.

5. Start the process by describing your own potato by saying 'My potato is brown' or lumpy, or knobbly, etc. Then either go round the group, or ask for volunteers.

6. When you have collected as many words as you can, say them together making a rhythmic word poem such as: 'Brown, brown, brown; lumpy, lumpy, lumpy; heavy; heavy; cold.'

7. Give them safe knives to cut their potatoes in half. Younger children may need help.

8. Look at the inside of the potatoes, smell them, touch them. *What do they feel like? Do they smell of anything? Are they wet or dry?* Take photos.

9. Now challenge the children to cut their potato into as many pieces as they can, and count them.

10. Put all the pieces in the big bowl or pan with some water and cook them.

11. When they are cooked look at how they have changed from hard to soft. Mash the potatoes with some milk and a little butter, and let the children try their own mashed potato.

Taking it forward

- Make cooking a real shared experience by exploring a whole pumpkin, and making pumpkin soup together.

What's in it for the children?

Scientific processes: Living things (plants), changes through heating.

Fascinating fact: Cooking breaks down the cell walls in the potatoes.

Magic marks
Investigate a box of candles

What you need:

- A camera
- A clipboard
- A box of white 'household' candles
- Coloured candles
- One candle in a safe candle holder
- Matches
- Smooth, thin white paper
- White boards or pastry boards
- Small containers, such as saucers or small yogurt pots
- Runny paint
- Cotton wool balls

Taking it forward

■ Try grating some old wax crayons and sprinkling the gratings between two sheets of paper. Cover the paper with a couple of sheets of newspaper and iron them with a warm (not hot!) iron (adult only). Peep between the sheets to see what is happening and iron again if necessary.

What's in it for the children?

Scientific processes: Exploring materials, melting, changes through heating.

Fascinating fact: Wax makes the paper resistant to the water in the paint.

Health & Safety

Always keep matches out of reach, and warn children never to touch them.

What to do:

1. Help the children to collect all the things you need. Appoint a photographer and make sure they know what to do. Don't let them miss out on the activity.

2. Sit together and look at the materials you are going to use.

3. Light your demonstration candle and watch it until it starts to melt. *What are candles made from? What is that bit sticking out of the top called? Why is it there? Why is the candle melting? What is running down the candle?* Blow the candle out before you continue your exploration.

4. Pass the other candles round the group so the children can feel them as they discuss their properties, encourage new vocabulary such as smooth, shiny, waxy, slippery.

5. Now ask the children: *Could you use a candle like a pencil to make marks on paper? Would the marks show?*

6. Give them some paper so they can try it out, talking about what is happening as they work. Offer some coloured candles too.

7. Encourage them to draw and scribble all over the paper so the paper is covered with plenty of wax.

8. Now show the children how to use the paint on a cotton ball to paint the paper all over. *What is happening? Why do you think the paint doesn't cover all the paper?*

Top tip ⭐
You could use any candle ends you may have, or ask families to donate them for this activity.

What you need:

- A camera
- A clipboard
- Three packets of cornflour
- Trays or shallow boxes
- Magnifying glasses
- Spoons
- Water in a small plastic bottle
- Cooking oil in a small plastic bottle
- A can of non-allergenic shaving foam
- Three plastic bowls

Top tip ★

It's easier to do a controlled science experiment if you use a packet for each mixture. Bargain food stores sell cheap cornflour.

Taking it forward

Help the children to make their own dough of all sorts, the preparation gives an ideal time to use simple scientific vocabulary about materials and how they change.

What's in it for the children?

Scientific processes: Materials, change through adding liquids, making hypotheses (guesswork).

Fascinating fact: Scientists are still puzzled about the way cornflour particles clump together when you compress or hit them, but then go liquid again.

➕ Health & Safety

Buy non-allergenic shaving foam.

What to do:

1. Help the children to collect all the things you need.

2. Ask the children why they think you need three packets of cornflour. Explain that you are going to be scientists and to do an experiment, so you must be careful to have equal amounts in each of your experiment to make it fair. *What does 'fair' mean?* Check on the packets that they contain the same amounts.

3. Now look at the liquids you are using, and talk about each one. Explain that foam is a liquid with lots of air bubbles in it.

4. Help the children to tip a packet of cornflour into each of the bowls. Put one of the liquids next to each bowl. *What do you think will happen when we add some water? Or some oil? Or squirt some foam in?*

5. Start with just one bowl and let the children add water to the cornflour a spoonful at a time, while another child stirs. Count the spoonfuls and look at the mixture as it turns into classic cornflour 'gloop'. Let the children scoop the mixture with their fingers as they describe what it feels like.

6. Take the next bowl and slowly add some cooking oil to the cornflour, using a spoon so you can measure the same number of spoonfuls as the first mixture. Ask the children to mix and knead this one with their hands so it turns into a soft, smooth dough. *What does this mixture feel like? Is it the same or different from the first one?*

7. Now take the final bowl and ask a child to add a good squirt of shaving foam, mixing with a spoon or their hands. You need slightly more shaving foam than cornflour, and if you keep kneading this one, it will turn into cloud-like soft dough. *What does this mixture look and feel like?*

8. Put the three bowls where you can all see them, and talk about the different mixtures you have made. Take some photos.

Popping science

Investigate a packet of popcorn kernels

What you need:

- A camera
- A clipboard
- A bag or box of popping corn (plain not sweetened)
- A saucepan with a lid, or a microwaveable bowl and a plastic plate
- Magnifying glasses, spoons, water in a jug or plastic bottle
- Small bowls or yogurt pots and spoons
- Access to a stove or microwave

Top tip

Bargain shops and supermarkets have popping corn.

Taking it forward

- Do some experiments with other dried vegetables – peas, beans, lentils or chickpeas, watching what happens as they soak. Talk about how they get bigger. What is happening?

What's in it for the children?

Scientific processes: Foods in their natural states, drying foods, effects of heat on objects.

Fascinating fact: Popcorn kernels are damp inside, and when the kernels get hot, the water expands and pops the hard shell of the corn.

✚ Health & Safety

Check for any allergies or intolerances. Children who are wheat intolerant can often eat sweetcorn products safely, but check with parents.

What to do:

1. Help the children to collect all the things you need. Appoint a photographer.

2. Sit together and pass the packet of corn around. *Do you know what this is? Have you ever eaten popcorn? How do you make it? Why is it called popcorn?*

3. Look at any pictures on the packet and help the children to read the information – including the weight, the ingredients, and the instructions for cooking. Talk about what sweetcorn is. *How does sweetcorn grow? Have you eaten sweetcorn? What does it taste like?* They may talk about tinned corn, corn on the cob, or even nachos.

4. Tip a small amount of the corn (not the whole pack) into tray or a small bowl and pass it round for the children to investigate, using magnifying glasses if they like. *Why are the kernels so hard? What do you think has happened to them? How can you turn such hard things into popcorn?* Some children may already know!

5. Now read out the instructions for making popcorn, and follow them, making sure that children are well away from anything hot, but near enough to hear the 'pops'. Remind the children to listen for the popping sounds.

6. When the corn has all popped tip it out into little bowls or pots. *How has the corn changed? What made it change?*

7. Let the children try some it if they want to.

Swirly whirly
Investigate colour mixing

What you need:

- A camera
- A clipboard
- **Whole milk** (skimmed milk doesn't work for this exploration)
- **Enough larger bowls so everyone can see what happens on the surface of the milk**
- **Artificial food colouring**
- **Small bowls or yogurt pots**
- **Washing-up liquid**
- **Plastic droppers or pipettes**

Top tip ⭐

Shop-bought artificial food colouring is stronger than natural food colouring, so it will work better.

Taking it forward

- Ask the children if the swirly experiment would work with other liquids – water, juice, skimmed milk. Try some.

What's in it for the children?

Scientific processes: Changes, liquids and solids, floating and sinking.

Fascinating fact: The fat and protein molecules in the milk mix with the washing-up liquid and make them move around on the surface. They will eventually sink, as the fat, protein and soap are all mixed up.

✚ Health & Safety
Just because it has milk in it doesn't mean it's good to drink!

What to do:

1. Help the children to collect all the things you need. Appoint a photographer, and get ready to do some filming – video clips will really capture this exploration.

2. Pour some milk into each of the larger bowls, and talk with the children about milk. *Where does milk come from? Why is it important to drink milk?*

3. Take the discussion further if the children are interested. *Is milk a liquid, like water? Could you swim in a bath of milk? Could you float a boat on the surface? What sort of object could float on the milk? What would sink?*

4. Tell the children you are going to see how you can make colours float on the can surface of the milk. Look at the food colouring. *Do you think the food colouring will float or sink?*

5. Use droppers to carefully drop colouring onto the surface of the milk. It should float. Use several colours to make a drippy pattern.

6. Now very carefully drop a few drops of washing-up liquid onto the colouring – watch what happens. The colours will swirl and move around on the surface of the milk.

7. Talk about what you can see. *Why do the children think this is happening?*

8. If the swirling slows down, add a bit more washing-up liquid. The swirling should last for at least ten minutes.

9. Talk about what's happening.

Underneath

Investigate a log

What you need:

- A camera
- A clipboard
- A log, an old plank or a piece of guttering
- Some bug collectors or 'pooters'
- Magnifying glasses, tweezers, cocktail sticks or straws
- Plastic trays
- A sheet or blanket to sit on

What to do:

1. Help the children to collect all the things you need. Appoint a photographer or even two for this lively exploration.

2. Sit together near the log and talk about what you are going to do. You could call yourselves explorers or David Attenborough's helpers, going to look for new living things.

3. Remind the children that they may find insects or other living creatures under the log or elsewhere in the garden. The naturalists' rule is that minibeasts must be collected and handled very carefully, and put back in the place where you found them. They are very fragile and can be damaged easily, so take care when you pick them up so you don't injure them. Never squash or stamp on a minibeast.

4. Make sure the children know how to use the bug catchers, insect pots and magnifying glasses, showing them if necessary.

5. Ask them what they think you will find under the log. *Do they think there will be living things? What sort? Can they name some of the creatures they might find?*

6. Help the children to carefully and slowly lift the log from the ground and turn it over. Keep very still and watch for movements. *What can you see? Can you carefully capture some of the minibeasts?*

Top tip ⭐

Several days before doing this activity, either locate a good log or just leave a piece of wood or guttering in a quiet corner outside so it has time to attract some minibeasts.

50 fantastic ideas for investigations

7. You may find little spiders, worms, slugs, ants, woodlice, earwigs or centipedes. Tell the children that the minibeasts they find won't hurt them and are probably more frightened of them! Look together at what you find, naming each creature. Look at legs, bodies, wings, feelers.

8. Take plenty of photos of the minibeasts you find.

9. When you have finished your exploration, carefully turn the log back over and gently replace the minibeasts close to it where they can crawl back to safety. The children can return to look for more minibeasts later.

10. When you go indoors you can print the photos so children can draw or talk about your under a log adventure.

Taking it forward
- Put some dead leaves and damp soil in a terrarium or empty aquarium and keep some of the minibeasts for a single day before returning them to their habitat.

What's in it for the children?
Scientific processes: Living things; minibeasts.

Fascinating fact: Most bugs and other minibeasts help us by eating rotted plant material.

➕ Health & Safety
Some children are frightened of bugs, and may become uncontrolled or noisy. Explain what is going to happen and give extra attention to frightened children. Remind children to wash their hands carefully afterwards.

What's in it?
Investigate plastic containers

What you need:

- A camera
- A clipboard
- Empty water tray
- **Plastic containers in lots of different sizes** (five or six will do), **and a variety of shapes** (oblong, square, round) **watertight, and without holes in the bottoms**
- A plastic jug or bottle of tap water and a funnel
- A variety of small measuring tools: plastic spoons of different sizes, cups, yogurt pots
- A measuring jug marked in millilitres (ml)

:Top tip ⭐

Add a few drops of food colouring to the water to make it easier to see levels.

Taking it forward

- Try the same exploration with rice or sand instead of water.
- Take the bucket challenge. Guess first and then check how many yogurt pots of water it takes to fill a plastic bucket.

What's in it for the children?

Scientific processes: Capacity, measures.

Fascinating fact: Capacity is one of the most difficult science concepts to teach, as well as to learn!

What to do:

1. Collect all the things you need and appoint a photographer. Make sure they know that they can decide what to photograph.

2. Investigate together the containers you've collected and talk about them.

3. Ask the children to guess which container will hold the most and which the least. Put these two at opposite ends of the water tray.

4. Help the children to arrange the other containers in order of their volume, between them.

5. *Can you think of a way to check whether we are right?* Try their suggestions until they find a way that works. If they haven't already thought of it, suggest using the water and the measuring jug.

6. Review the result. *Was our arrangement right? If not, why not? Was it to do with the different shapes of the containers? Do some shapes look bigger than others of the same volume?*

7. Choose a medium size container and remove the others from the water tray. Show the children the measuring tools (spoons, cups, pots, etc.) and let each child (or pair) choose one to try.

8. Now pose a challenge. *Can you guess how many of your measuring tools it will take to fill the container? Write down your estimates, then take turns to have a go. Were you right?*

9. Try again with one of the other measuring tools. Children should get better at estimating as they go on, but capacity is a very difficult concept for children to understand.

10. Have a look at some standard measuring vessels, such as a measuring jug, measuring cups or spoons, and talk about the marks and what they mean. Young children need plenty of practice with non-standard measures such as spoons, cups, and bottles, before using standard measures.

Mudlarks

nvestigate mud and clay

What you need:

- A camera
- A clipboard
- Two large, empty trays or plastic containers
- A small bucket of dry garden soil (sieved to remove stones)
- A pack or lump of clay
- A plastic jug or cup and a bottle of water
- Small items (toys, keys, buttons, coins) to press in the soil or clay

What to do:

1. Collect all the things you need and appoint a photographer.

2. Tip the soil into the dry water tray. Encourage the children to explore it with their hands. Help them to find words to describe what it feels like (powdery, coarse, gritty, dusty). *Where does soil come from? What is it made from? What is in it?*

3. Try to make a ball of soil with your hands. *Will it hold together? Can you make an impression or marks in it using a toy or a coin? Why can't you make things with it?* The children will probably know that it's too dry.

4. Use the jug or cup to add some water, a little at a time Mix it in, and pause at each stage to examine what difference the water has made.

5. When you feel the consistency is right, try again making impressions with the toy cars, keys, etc. *What happens now?*

6. Put the damp clay in the other tray, keeping it separate from the soil. Encourage the children to examine it, squashing, squeezing, moulding, stretching. *What is clay? Where does it come from? How is it different from clay?*

7. Use the keys, coins, etc. to make impressions in the clay. *Which takes impressions best, the soil or the clay? Can anybody suggest why?*

8. Go back to the soil and add more water so it is really wet. Mix it in. *Will the soil take an impression now? Why not?*

Taking it forward

- Talk about the value of soil for plants. Take two small plants, such as daisies or dandelions from your garden. Try to choose ones that are as near identical as you can get. Plant one in soil and one in clay. Which does best? Do the children have any theories why?

- Go out after rain and see if the children can find any tracks in the mud. Photograph them and try to identify what they are.

What's in it for the children?

Scientific processes: Properties of materials, changes, wet/dry.

Fascinating fact: Soil is the 'skin of the earth'. It is made of mixtures of minerals, water, air, organic matter and organisms that are the decaying remains of once-living things.

✚ Health & Safety

Garden soil is generally safe, so long as it's kept out of mouths, and hands are washed afterwards. If you are worried, use peat free compost from a garden centre.

Top tip ★

Make sure the soil is really dry before you start - the drier the better. Leave it on a sunny windowsill, or dry it in an oven (not a microwave).

Quaint paint

Investigate paint

What you need:

- A camera
- A clipboard
- Water
- Any single colour of powder paint (unmixed)
- A selection of things that will mix with the paint (sugar, sand, milk, juice, paste, coffee)
- A tray
- One large container to mix the paint
- Smaller containers for the exploration
- A roll of lining paper
- Paintbrushes

Top tip

Include some things, such as instant coffee, cocoa, conditioner, which will change the colour and smell of the paint as well as the texture.

Taking it forward

- Experiment with the mixes using different mark makers: brushes, modelling sticks, cotton buds, etc. and marking on different surfaces including wood, glass, stone and tile.

What's in it for the children?

Scientific processes: Properties of materials, changes.

Fascinating fact: You can make your own powder paint by crushing coloured chalk with a hammer.

What to do:

1. Collect all the things you need and appoint a photographer.

2. Talk with the children about the powder paint. *What does the powder look and feel like? What other things is it like? How do you make it into paint?*

3. Children will say, mix with water, so do that. Don't make it too thin – about the consistency of yogurt is fine. Mix a fair quantity (several children can have a go to make sure it is thoroughly mixed).

4. Let the children experiment with the paint by making marks on the surface you've chosen.

5. Pour paint into some of the smaller containers. Look at the other things you have on the tray. Ask the children what they would like to add to the paint to make it different. Treat all suggestions seriously and try them by mixing and making marks on the chosen surface. As you go along, label each container and each group of marks according to what's been mixed with the paint.

6. Discuss each mix. *Does the paint look or work differently when things are added? Is it different mixed with paste? Or milk? Or coffee?*

7. Help and encourage the children to describe how the mixed paint looks and feels. *Is it thicker or thinner? Has it changed colour?*

8. Line up the labelled containers, and let a child chose one. *Can we separate the paint from the sand, coffee or glue? How would we do this?* Try some of the suggestions – these may include using sieves, colanders, or even coffee filters.

9. Talk about why some mixtures can be separated and some can't – use words such as dissolve, disappear, invisible.

What you need:

- A camera
- A clipboard
- A bag of old T-shirts
- Sharp scissors
- Magnifying glasses
- Tape measures

Top tip ⭐

Ask families for old clean T-shirts, it doesn't matter if they are very old, just clean!

Taking it forward

- As the children grow taller, you can make the 'laser strings' higher to challenge them further.

What's in it for the children?

Scientific processes: Materials, classification, changes through deconstruction.

Fascinating fact: T-shirts are knitted, so they are more stretchy than woven fabrics.

What to do:

1. Help the children to collect all the things you need. Appoint a photographer.

2. Tip out the bag of T-shirts on the carpet or a table. Let the children look at them to see what you have.

3. *How can we sort these T-shirts?* Listen carefully to what they suggest and try more than one way: size, colour, sleeves/no sleeves, men's/women's/children's, logos/no logos etc. Be sure to only sort by one set of criteria at a time, and give plenty of time for discussion.

4. Now look more carefully at the T-shirts and sort out any that have no seams down the sides. This will make the rest of the investigation much easier.

5. Show the children how to start at the bottom of the body of the T-shirt and cut with scissors - all the way along the hem, then without cutting this bit off, continue cutting in a sort of spiral round and round the shirt. You should get a very long length of stretchy 'string'. If the children cut shorter lengths by mistake, just knot the ends and keep cutting. Younger children may need help, or might prefer to just watch!

6. Keep cutting until you get to the armholes, then stop. Cut off your string, and continue with other T-shirts until you have a big pile of strings.

7. Let the children test how stretchy the string is, and talk about how you have changed the T-shirts into something else.

8. Now tie all your strings together and take them outside where you can test them by pulling toys around or having a 'safe' tug-of-war.

9. Make a 'laser beam' game by tying the strings low down near the ground, from trees to apparatus, to bushes and fences. You will be surprised how much string you have made. Let the children play stepping between the strings without touching any of them.

 **Health & Safety**

Blunt scissors cause more accidents than sharp ones. Teach children to use all tools properly, particularly ones with sharp edges. It's better to have a smaller number of good scissors than a lot of frustrating blunt pairs!

What floats your boat?

Investigate floating and sinking

What you need:

- A camera
- A clipboard
- Water
- Three trays or other containers
- A large and fairly deep watertight container, such as a plastic storage box, baby bath, or a wide bucket
- Some things that might float, and might sink (wooden blocks, modelling tools, lollipop sticks, plastic bottles with tops on, plastic cars or boats)

What to do:

1. Collect all the things you need and appoint a photographer.

2. Fill the container with water.

3. Gather the children in a circle and explain that you are going to investigate floating and sinking.

4. Ask them to go round the room with a partner, and collect in their hands, something they think will float in the water tray and something they think will sink. Remind them that the things must be waterproof, so no books, puzzle pieces or cardboard boxes!

5. Just give them a few minutes, and help anyone who seems lost or unfocused.

6. Sit down in a circle again, and with a friend use 'talk partnering' to discuss the things they have found and what they think each one will do when they are put in the water. Ask a few of the children to show the whole group their objects and tell their predictions.

7. Put the three trays by the water container and label one 'float', the next 'sink' and the third '?'. *Why have I written a question mark on the third one?*

Top tip

There can be quite a lot of splashing – protect the floor, or do it outside.

8. Now the children can test their theories by putting their chosen objects in the water, watching what happens and then putting the object on the right tray. Some objects will need to go on the '?' tray because they either float just under the surface or sink and then float.

9. Photograph what happens. *Were your guesses right? Was there anything you expected to sink/float but didn't? Can you make up any rules for floating and sinking? Does it only depend on how heavy a thing is?*

10. Experiment with some of the objects you have collected yourself to see what happens to them. Ask the children to predict what will happen to each of your objects.

11. Ask some floating and sinking questions: *Could you make a plastic bottle sink? Can you make a wooden block sink by putting something heavy on it? Can you make an empty margarine tub float? Can you make it sink? Do all heavy objects sink? Do all light objects float?*

Taking it forward

- Introduce some scales and weigh the objects before you test them.

- Make a collection of pictures of things that float.

What's in it for the children?

Scientific processes: Forces, floating and sinking.

Fascinating fact: Some things will float just under the surface. This is usually called submerged – neither floating nor sinking.

Can I help you?

Investigate a box of shoes

What you need:

- A camera
- A clipboard
- A box of good condition adults' and children's shoes of all sorts and sizes
- A roll of paper
- Big felt pens, scissors
- Magnifying glasses
- Simple tape measure, marked in centimetres

Top tip

Charity shops and the children's own families are a good source of outgrown shoes. Discard any that are broken or otherwise undesirable or dangerous.

Taking it forward

- Use the shoes to make a role play shoe shop, with chairs, shop assistants, a low-level mirror and carrier bags to take the shoes home.

What's in it for the children?

Scientific processes: Materials, classifying.

Fascinating fact: Shoes that are too small alter the shape of children's bones for ever!

Health & Safety

Include adult shoes, but not very high heels as children may twist their ankles when trying to walk in them.

What to do:

1. Help the children to collect all the things you need. Appoint a photographer and make sure they know what to do.

2. Tip the shoes out on the carpet, indoors or outside, and let the children explore them freely. Of course, they will want to try them on!

3. When they have investigated the shoes ask the children some open questions such as: *Why do we need shoes? What are shoes made from? How are shoes made? How do you find out what size a pair of shoes is? Are there special shoes for wearing on holiday, or to a party?*

4. Now suggest that the shoes need sorting – *How could they be sorted?* Listen carefully, they may come up with some novel ideas. You could sort them:

   - by size, largest to smallest
   - by age group (babies', children's, men's women's)
   - by colour
   - by fastening (buckles, laces, Velcro)
   - by material (leather, fabric, plastic)
   - by occasion (party, work, holiday, school).

5. Unroll some paper and draw circles to help the sorting, or so that children can line up the shoes in size. Take some photos! Then sort them again a different way. Are there any shoes that don't fit their sorting criteria? Why don't they fit?

6. Choose one of the shoes and take it apart – undo the stitches and separate the shoe upper from the sole. Talk about the different parts: sole, tongue, upper, lace, heel, toe. Flatten the upper and look at how the shape changes when it is flat. Why is this? How could we put the shoe back together again?

What you need:

- A camera
- A clipboard
- Two small buckets or bowls
- Water: soft water or bottled water makes better bubbles
- Washing-up liquid
- A small bowl, a cup measure
- Glycerine
- Lots of bubble blowers

Top tip ⭐

Get glycerine from a chemist, or online.

What to do:

1. Help the children to collect all the things you need. Appoint a photographer – they will be busy photographing bubbles before they burst!

2. Make some bubble liquid in one of the buckets – ten cups of water to one cup of washing-up liquid. Mix well with a stick or spoon.

3. Pour some of the bubble mixture into a little bowl and hand it round so everyone can look at it. *How is the mixture different from water? What makes it different?* Encourage the use of language such as gloopy, slimy, thick.

4. Make sure you have enough bubble wands for everyone – you will need lots! You can make more bubble blowers from pipe cleaners, soft garden wire, or coat hangers bent into shapes.

5. Use your bubble wands to make bubbles and watch them carefully. *How do you make a big bubble? How do you make a stream of small bubbles? What makes the bubble move? What is inside the bubbles? What makes the colours on the surface of the bubbles?*

6. Gather the children together and show them the bottle of glycerine. Look at it in the bottle and tip the bottle around so they can see how thick the glycerine is. Ask the children what they think will happen if you add some of the glycerine to some new bubble mixture.

7. Put ten cups of water in the second bucket, add a cup of washing-up liquid. Stir well. Add two to three tablespoons of glycerine and stir again.

8. Make some bubbles with this mixture. *Is this mixture better, worse, or just the same?* It should be better!

9. Ask the children why they think the second mixture is better.

10. Blow bubbles and try to catch them on your wand, or on a dry finger, or a wet finger. Talk about what happens.

Taking it forward

- Try making different shaped bubble wands and see if you can blow different shaped bubbles with them.

What's in it for the children?

Scientific processes: Changes, surface tension.

Fascinating fact: Glycerine makes the surface of the bubbles stronger.

✚ Health & Safety

Soap makes some surfaces slippery, take care.

Shelly times
Investigate a box of eggs

What you need:

- A camera
- A clipboard
- A box of six hens' eggs
- One or two hard boiled eggs
- Small plastic bowls and a small plastic tray or plate
- Magnifying glasses
- Small saucepan or microwaveable bowl and wooden spoon
- Forks and spoons, a small amount of milk
- Access to a stove or microwave

Top tip ⭐

Have an empty egg carton ready for some of the eggs so you can pass two boxes round more quickly, and everyone has a turn.

What to do:

1. Help the children to collect all the things you need. Appoint a photographer.

2. Sit together and look at the box of eggs. Some children may never have done this before, so go slowly and make sure everyone can see.

3. Pass the whole box of eggs carefully round the group (this is safer than passing a single egg). Let the children gently take an egg from the box and hold it in their hand before returning it to the box and passing it to their neighbour (see hint above). *What are eggs? Where do they come from? Are all eggs laid by birds? Why are the eggs different colours?*

4. When everyone has examined an egg, ask for a volunteer to break an egg into a bowl. Younger children will need help, and it's best to put the bowl on a tray to catch spills. Put the eggshell on the tray beside the bowl.

5. Carefully pass the tray around so everyone can see what was in the eggshell. Look at the inside of the eggshell as well as the white and yolk of the egg. *Do you know what the yellow bit of the egg is called? What is the yellow part for?* Explain that it is food for the baby chick, which grows inside the egg if it is left with the mother hen.

- Tip an egg onto a plastic plate so they can see the yolk and white, and gently touch them with a finger. *Do you know why the transparent part is called the 'white'?* Show the children the hard-boiled egg, and explain that you have cooked it in water still in its shell. Peel the egg and cut it open so the children can see why we call the outer part the 'white'.

- Explain that you are going to cook your eggs in a different way. Let the children carefully mix the eggs with forks until the whites and yolks are all mixed, adding some more eggs if you need to. Pour all the eggs into one bowl and add a little milk.

- Make scrambled eggs in a pan or the microwave (remember to use a plastic bowl in the microwave).

- Make sure the eggs are cool enough to eat before using teaspoons to taste the scrambled eggs, encouraging describing words as you talk about how they have changed.

Taking it forward

■ Take a trip to the supermarket with the children to see how many different sorts and sizes of eggs they can find.

What's in it for the children?

Scientific processes: Living things, changes through heating.

Fascinating fact: Hens' eggs are different colours, because different birds eat different foods and so the shells come out different colours.

 Health & Safety

Wipe the eggs thoroughly before handling them with the children. Check for allergies.

All strung up

Investigate string

What you need:

- A camera
- A clipboard
- Several balls of string – different colours of cotton string would be best
- Scissors (several pairs)
- Felt pens
- Sticky labels
- A display board and drawing pins or tacks

Top tip

Children get better at measuring by doing it. Give plenty of opportunities to practice.

Taking it forward

- Hang the string measures on the wall, with the children's names and photographs. Use them again in a few weeks to see if anyone has grown, and by how much.

What's in it for the children?

Scientific processes: comparisons, measurement.

Fascinating fact: Give plenty of practice with these 'non-standard' measures before using standard measures such as rulers.

Health & Safety

No special issues, but watch for children getting entangled in the string.

What to do:

1. Collect all the things you need and appoint a photographer to record your investigation.

2. Gather the children in a group and put a ball of string in front of them. Ask them what string is for. You'll get a variety of ideas, such as tying people up, doing up a parcel, making a clothes line, hanging things up. After some discussion, if it hasn't been suggested, ask if you could use string for measuring.

3. Group the children in pairs. Give each pair a length of string, a marker and a pair of scissors, and challenge them to use these to measure and compare their heights

4. Let them experiment, and only help them if they are really stuck. Watch what they do, and draw attention to any particularly effective methods. One way is for one child to lie down while the other puts a line of string alongside him/her and marks on it the position of the feet and the head, then cutting it to the marked length. However, there are lots of other ways! Make sure the other child in the pair is measured too. Make sure you involve the photographer.

5. As soon as everyone has been measured, the children can label their strings with their names, using sticky labels bent round the string. By the end of the exercise each child should have a piece of string, which is a measurement of their height and labelled with their name

6. Lay out the strings on the floor and see which is longest.

7. Use a new piece of string to measure round each other's heads. Compare the strings, and name them.

8. Use these strings to find objects that are longer or shorter round than their own head. They could try boxes, tins, bottles, other body parts, other children's heads – investigate out of doors as well.

What you need:

- A camera
- A clipboard
- Resources to make sloping runs: plastic guttering, planks of wood, strips of rigid plastic, tubes of various sorts, an indoor slide
- Things to support the runs: plastic crates, chairs, stools
- Small balls of various types and weights: tennis, ping-pong, foam, marbles, large and small ball-bearings, air flow balls
- Some bricks of different shapes
- Other things of different shapes that will roll: toy cars, cotton reels, wooden and plastic cylinders
- Masking or duct tape

Top tip ⭐

You need plenty of space for this. Outdoors is best.

Taking it forward

- Make the run longer, and introduce some uphill sections, or a water chute (like a roller coaster). How do the objects behave on this new track?

What's in it for the children?

Scientific processes: Forces.

Fascinating fact: Objects will move faster on steeper slopes. Friction slows objects down.

What to do:

1. Collect all the things you need and appoint a photographer to record your work.

2. Work with the children to construct a ramp and some tracks for rolling off the end, using the guttering, tubes and other items you've collected, and the crates/chairs/ stools to support them. Make the tracks are various heights, lengths and gradients. Don't make them too steep.

3. Tape the joints to make them firm. You could tape the more elaborate ones to the supports.

4. If you've used planks or flat plastic strips, try making some side-pieces to stop things falling off the edges.

5. Now ask the children to think: *How could we test the ramp?* You could have a rolling race, but take their suggestions if they have some.

6. Look at the balls first, and ask the children which ball they think will be the best roller. Talk about what being 'best roller' means: *Is the best roller the one that goes furthest? The one that goes fastest? The heaviest one? The biggest one? The one that stays in the middle of the track?* You need to agree.

7. Put the balls in order of popularity for best rolling. Take a photo.

8. Start the test by holding each ball in turn at the top of the track and letting go. Mark where the ball stops. Continue with each ball in turn, and put them in another line at the bottom of the slope according to their success.

9. *Were your guesses/estimations right? Can you say why some objects roll down the track more successfully than others?*

10. Now try the same thing with the bricks, the cotton reels, model cars, etc. *Why do some of these roll down more successfully than others?*

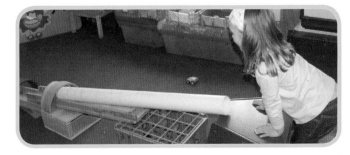

Magic reflections

Investigate mirrors

What you need:

- A camera
- A clipboard
- Small unbreakable mirrors (ideally the size of individual white boards)
- Paint in small pots, mixed with a small amount of moisturiser to help it stick
- Short, small brushes or cotton buds

Top tip ⭐

Search online for small unbreakable mirrors. Offer 'skin' and 'hair' colours for self portraits.

Taking it forward

- Use this method to paint unusual pictures by putting the mirror on the floor under a tree, under a table, or reflecting unusual objects.

What's in it for the children?

Scientific processes: Light, colour, reflection.

Fascinating fact: A mirror image is a reflected duplication of an object that appears almost identical, but is reversed.

Health & Safety

Children should be taught not to reflect the sun in hand-held mirrors.

What to do:

1. Help the children to collect all the things you need. Appoint a photographer.

2. Sit together and explain that today you are going to investigate reflections. *Do you know what a reflection is?*

3. Let every child (or pair of children) take a mirror and use it to investigate the environment of your setting, indoors and outside. Remind them to use the mirror to look at things below their feet and above their heads as well as at their eye level.

4. After a period of free exploration, sit together again and talk about what they found out. *Did the world look different?* What happens if they look at writing or numbers in a mirror? Hopefully someone may have found that mirrors reverse images, and you can talk about this.

5. Now get the children to look closely at their own faces in the mirrors. *What can you see? Where are your eyebrows? Your eyelashes?* Go round the group and ask each child to say something about her or himself, 'I have brown curly hair,' 'My lips are pinky brown,' etc. Praise the use of sentences and describing words.

6. Prop the mirrors up (if they are working in pairs, let one child hold the mirror for their friend) and use cotton buds or small paintbrushes to paint a self-portrait on the surface of the mirror, following the lines and colours they see.

7. Take photos of the portraits, and then wash the mirrors for someone else to have a go.

Make your mark

Investigate mark makers

What you need:

- A camera
- A clipboard
- A large collection of pens, pencils, crayons, felt pens, markers, paintbrushes, dabbers, small sponges
- Paint in small trays
- A roll of plain, thick paper, such as lining paper
- Masking tape or duct tape
- White glue in small pots

Top tip

This is a good opportunity to use up all those 'nearly dry' markers and felt pens, just dip them in a pot of water, or take the inner sleeve out for a short life extension.

Taking it forward

- Try painting slightly diluted white glue all over opened-out plastic bags. Drop glitter, small seeds and sequins on the wet glue and when it's dry, carefully peel the glittery and now clear glue sheet off the plastic. What has happened?

What's in it for the children?

Scientific processes: Materials, changes through mixing, diluting, drying.

Fascinating fact: The name 'felt pen' comes from the hard felt that is used as the tip.

What to do:

1. Collect all the things you need. Appoint a photographer, and make sure they know what they need to do.

2. Help the children to cover a long table, or a part of the floor with paper. Stick it firmly to the table, or hold it down to the floor with tape or big bricks.

3. Now gather round and have a look at all the mark makers you have collected. Focus on the ends of the markers, and talk about their shapes, 'thick', 'thin', 'sloping', 'fuzzy', 'spongy' etc.

4. Explain to the children that you are going to investigate the marks these tools make, not by drawing a picture, but by making different marks. This may be an unfamiliar activity, as children are usually encouraged to draw figuratively.

5. Start experimenting on the paper to see how many different ways you can use each marker, working freely all over the paper, making dots, dabs, wiggles and lines. Talk about these marks as you work.

6. Now try drips and drops of water, white glue or runny paint on the marks you have made. *What happens as the liquid meets the felt pen marks?*

7. Leave the markers and the paper out all day and see what happens as children return to the activity to add more marks or watch what is happening as the paper dries in some places, and gets wet in others.

8. Visit the marks with children and talk about what has happened as their own marks get covered, or dissolved by others. Use words such as 'dissolve', 'change', 'liquid', 'mix', 'shiny', 'dry'.

9. Try leaving your mark making exploration outside in the rain or overnight.

Stick with it

Investigate glue and paste

What you need:

- A camera
- A clipboard
- A variety of glues and pastes: white glue, wallpaper paste, glue stick, flour and water paste, sticky tape, duct tape, masking tape
- Plastic from carrier bags, sticks or garden canes
- Magnifying glasses, spoons
- Water in a small watering can
- Small bowls or yogurt pots and spoons
- Felt pens
- A teddy

Top tip ⭐

Buy white glue from DIY stores in gallon cans, it's much cheaper.

Taking it forward

- Try making full sized waterproof dens with plastic sheeting, canes and tape or pegs and clips – it's a great technological challenge.

What's in it for the children?

Scientific processes: Materials and properties, structures.

Fascinating fact: Waterproof objects can be submerged underwater. Water resistant objects can cope with rain, or an accidental dip in water.

Health & Safety

Never let young children play with superglue or hot glue guns.

What to do:

1. Help the children to collect all the things you need. Appoint a photographer.

2. Sit together and look at all the different sorts of adhesives and sticky tapes you have collected. Tell the children you are going to be scientists, testing glues to see which is best for which job.

3. Explain that Teddy really likes going walking in the country, but he often gets wet when it rains. He needs a tent to keep him dry, and he has tried to make one, but it leaks. Teddy is asking us to make one that is really waterproof.

4. These are the materials that Teddy has: plastic sheeting, some sticks and different sorts of glue and tape. He has asked the scientists to test the tent before he takes it, so he can be sure it is waterproof.

5. If you are working in a small group, the children could all work together, but a bigger group may need to work in smaller groups.

6. Let the children look at the resources you have collected and decide which they think will be the best for sticking Teddy's tent.

7. Write their ideas on the clipboard before they start working. Help the children if they need it, but try not to interfere as they make their structures – making mistakes is part of learning.

8. When the structures are finished, the children need to test them to be sure they are waterproof. They can do this outside using a small watering can, with Teddy inside the shelter.

9. Talk about what worked and what didn't, how they could improve the shelter, and whether they were right in guessing which adhesive would work best.

What you need:

- A camera
- A clipboard
- A big bag of pipe cleaners (you need plenty)
- Beads, ring pulls, pasta tubes and shapes with holes
- Playdough or Plasticene
- Felt pens or pencils, scissors
- Googly eyes, glue stick (optional)
- Ribbons and beads

Top tip

It's cheaper to buy big bags of pipe cleaners on the internet, we found bags of over 100 for less than £1, and even 1,000 for under £6!

Taking it forward

Get some three-core electrical wire. Adult only: strip the grey, white or black outside casing from the wire, you will find three separate wires inside, they will probably be red, black and green. Cut these with wire cutters and let the children use the wire to make sculptures. It's quite safe, easy to work with, and will hold its shape.

What's in it for the children?

Scientific processes: Properties of materials, changes through bending and squashing.

Fascinating fact: Most wire will stay in the shape you have bent it, most plastics won't because they have a built-in shape memory.

What to do:

1. Help the children to collect all the things you need. Appoint a photographer.

2. Tip the bag of pipe cleaners out on the table. Look at them and feel them. *What are they made from? What are they for? Why are they called pipe cleaners? How does a pipe cleaner work? Why don't we need them for cleaning pipes any more?*

3. Try making some spirals by winding the pipe cleaners round a pencil or felt pen. *What makes them stay in shape?*

4. Now experiment to see how to bend the pipe cleaners into shapes. *Which shapes can you make? Can you make letters? Or words?*

5. *Can you join them together? Can you make them stand up on their own?*

6. Try making a pair of glasses, a model bike, a little monster, or a caterpillar by threading pasta shapes or beads on, and bending the wire to make the caterpillar wiggle.

7. Now work together to make the biggest structure you can, using as many pipe cleaners as you can. Use playdough or Plasticene to anchor the structure, and thread beads or other objects with holes on the wires. *Can you make the structure go all the way across the table? Or across the carpet?*

8. Make some mobiles from pipe cleaners, decorate them with ribbons and beads and hang them up outside.

➕ Health & Safety

Pipe cleaners have wires inside, take care with eyes, ears and fingers.

Boxing clever

Investigate boxes and cartons

What you need:

- A camera
- A clipboard
- Cardboard boxes of various shapes and sizes – including cereal packets, gift boxes, and other packaging, small enough for the children to handle easily, but not too small to work with
- Scissors
- Thin card
- Pencils, thin markers.
- Glue, sticky tape and a stapler.

Top tip ⭐

The type of box is important. They need to be tough enough to withstand being taken apart, but not too thick and heavy for the children to handle.

✚ Health & Safety

Take care! Some boxes are held together by big sharp staples.

What to do:

1. Collect all the things you need and appoint a photographer.

2. Put out enough of the boxes you've collected for each child (or pair) to have one. Give them time to examine them, play with them, and investigate them.

3. Ask them what the boxes are made of. *Do you know what cardboard is? How is cardboard made?* (It's made from compressed paper.) *How is it different from paper?*

4. *What do you think the box would look like if you flattened it out?* Work together to draw the shape on a large sheet of paper or a white board, talking the children through, and following their ideas.

5. Work together to take the boxes apart. Stress that the children need to do it carefully without ripping the cardboard. You might need to show them how to ease glued joints apart without damaging them. Have a few extra boxes in reserve for the 'less-controlled' members of the group!

6. Photograph these stages.

7. When each box has been dismantled, spread it out. *Do the shapes they have match the shape you drew together? Where are the differences? Looking at it now, would the shape you all drew together work as a box? If not, why not?*

8. Let the children draw round their box shapes. Mark where it should be folded. They may need a ruler to get the lines straight.

9. Assemble the boxes, using glue and tape (and staples if needed) to hold them together. Photograph the stages of assembly.

10. *Does the box you have made look like the box you took apart? How is it different? How well would your box work?*

Take a simple box with a fold-over lid. Close it. Put a heavy weight (such as an iron or a bottle of water) on top of the box in the middle of the lid. Observe what happens. Now put the same weight on top of the box across a corner. Does the same thing happen? Why not?

What's in it for the children?

cientific processes: Materials, tructures, forces.

ascinating fact: The name for a shape hat can be built into a box or other 3D bject is a 'net'.

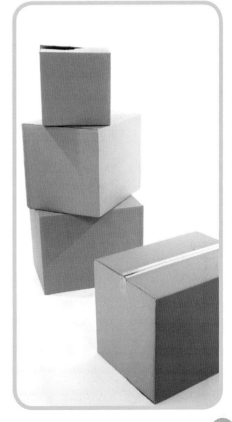

My stone, your stone
Investigate stones and pebbles

What you need:

- A camera
- A clipboard
- A bag of clean beach stones or garden stones, as varied as possible
- A roll of paper
- Scales or balance

Top tip

It is against local bye-laws in some places to take pebbles from beaches. If you can't find any then buy a small bag of pebbles from a garden centre.!

Taking it forward

■ Paint the stones with water to reveal their colours, then colour them, using a restricted palette of paints.

What's in it for the children?

Scientific processes: Materials, classification and ordering.

Fascinating fact: Stones and pebbles get their colours and patterns from the chemicals in the rock when they were formed.

 Health & Safety

Wash the stones before you use them.

What to do:

1. Help the children to collect all the things you need. Appoint a photographer.

2. Sit together on the carpet and pass the bag of pebbles round, so every child can choose one, and hold it safely in their hand. Remind them to be careful with stones and never throw them.

3. Now ask the children to examine their own pebble very carefully feeling its shape and texture, seeing its colours.

4. Now use 'talk partners' so the children can tell their partner about their pebble. Encourage them to use sentences: 'My pebble is…', 'My pebble feels…', 'My pebble is …colour'.

5. Go round the group taking turns to say one thing about each pebble (it's always alright for a child to miss a go, or repeat something another has said as long as it describes their stone too).

6. Now comes the hard bit – the children need to find out which is the heaviest of all the pebbles, not just the biggest! Using balance scales, help the children to work out how to find the heaviest pebble, probably by trial and error to start with until they come up with a system. Gradually eliminate and reduce the number. In a bigger group it would help to work with two balances and half the children to find the two heaviest, and younger children may just find the biggest one by ordering in a line.

7. Roll the paper out on the floor or a table and let all the children draw their own pebble on the same big picture, and 'have a go' at writing some words about its characteristics – colour, shape, texture etc.

Holes and tunnels

Investigate a bag of compost

What you need:

- A camera
- A clipboard
- A bag of compost – a sandy mix works best for this exploration
- A big plastic box, an empty water tray, or a builders' tray
- Magnifying glasses, spoons,
- Water in small plastic bottles
- Short lengths of drainpipe and guttering, plastic and cardboard tubes
- Cars and plastic boats

Top tip ⭐

Ask a carpet or fabric shop for the tubes from inside carpet rolls and fabrics, and saw these into lengths, and some lengths into halves lengthways to make bridges.

Taking it forward

- Read the book *The Tunnel* by Anthony Browne and replay the story in your setting, using a pop-up tunnel and fabrics.

What's in it for the children?

Scientific processes: Materials, structures.

Fascinating fact: All dead plants will rot down and decompose if you leave them alone, turning into a soil-like material called compost.

Health & Safety

Use a bag of sterilised compost from a garden centre.

What to do:

1. Help the children to collect all the things you need. Appoint a photographer.

2. Sit together and look at all the things you have collected.

3. Tip the compost into the box. Look at it and feel it with your hands, talking about how it looks and feels – dark, black, brown, gritty, trickling, sticky, lumpy etc. Use spoons and magnifying glasses, and talk about where compost comes from.

4. Now work together to make your compost into a mound in the box, talking as you work. If the compost rolls down and is too dry to make a stable hill, ask the children how you can make it stick together better. Children who have worked in the sand tray with dry and damp sand will know what you should do! Pour the water gently from bottles, a bit at a time, and don't add too much, or the tunnels will fall in.

5. Now ask the children for suggestions of ways that you could make tunnels through the hill you have made.

6. Look at the tubes and guttering you have collected.

7. Now try some of their ideas for making bridges and tunnels. Take plenty of photos of the ideas that don't work as well as those that do.

8. When you have made some tunnels and bridges, drive cars or boats through them.

9. *Can you make a tunnel with a bend in it? Or one that goes uphill?*

10. Continue your exploration by asking the children how you could make your hill into an island, or two islands. Sail some boats round the islands.

11. Make bridges between the islands and talk about which methods work and which ones don't.

12. Leave the islands for children to continue their explorations.

Tiny grainy stuff
Investigate sugar, salt and sand

What you need:

- A camera
- A clipboard
- Caster sugar, salt, sand in three bowls or other shallow containers of the same size
- A tray or shallow box
- A permanent marker pen and small pieces of card
- Circles of black paper, small plastic spoons
- Droppers, water in a plastic jug
- Magnifying glasses
- Transparent plastic pots with lids: spice jars, or baby food jars

Top tip ★
Dry, silver sand is best for comparison.

Taking it forward
- Put some icing sugar and water in a bottle, put on the lid tightly and shake it up. What happens to the sugar?

What's in it for the children?
Scientific processes: Mixing, separating, dissolving.

Fascinating fact: When something dissolves, it becomes a solution. When two substances are mixed without dissolving, they become a mixture.

Health & Safety
Tasting a very small amount of sand won't hurt any child, it's like being at a picnic on holiday!

What to do:

1. Help the children to collect all the things you need. Appoint a photographer.

2. Sit on the floor in a circle and put the bowls of sand, sugar and salt in the middle. Use the tray to reduce spillage.

3. Carefully pass each bowl round the group, looking at what is in each one, smelling and tasting (if they like). When you have all agreed what each one is, make a label for it – ask a child to do this.

4. Give each child a circle of black paper, and ask them to put it on the floor in front of them. Choose which substance to look at first. Let each child carefully spoon a little of it onto their paper and look at it through a magnifying glass. What can they see?

5. Now spoon a little of the next substance onto the paper next to the first. Look at this one: *What can you see? Is it different? How?*

6. Spoon some from the last bowl and look at all three. Talk about *same* and *different*.

7. Now use droppers to drop water, a drop at a time, onto each of the different substances. *What happens? Where did the stuff go?* Talk about dissolving.

8. Put a spoonful of salt in one jar, sand in the next and sugar in the third. Add some water, and screw on the tops. Write the contents on each jar. Let the children take turns to shake the jars and watch what happens. Talk about the differences between the jars, and where the sand and salt have gone. *Can we get the salt, sand or sugar out of the water again? How could you do it?*

Rocket launch
investigate a box of drinking straws

What you need:

- A camera
- A clipboard
- A box of plastic drinking straws
- A tray
- Some scrap paper
- A pack of sticky notes – rectangular ones are best
- Playground chalk

Taking it forward

- Make a blow football game in a shoebox or plastic storage box, using straws and ping pong balls.

What's in it for the children?

Scientific processes: Forces, air.

Fascinating fact: Before there were plastic straws, or even paper ones, people used pieces of straw from the fields to drink through.

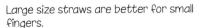

Top tip ⭐

Large size straws are better for small fingers.

What to do:

1. Help the children to collect all the things you need. Appoint a photographer.

2. Tip out the straws onto the tray, and look at them together. Does anyone know why they are called straws?

3. Ask the children how they could use the straws to make things move without touching them. Try some of their ideas, using bits of torn paper. *How far can you make the paper move? If you blow harder, does the paper go further? Is it easier with big pieces or small pieces? Is it better on the carpet or the floor?*

4. Ask them if they know what is making the paper move. (It's the force of the air that makes the paper move – blow harder and the paper goes further and faster.)

5. Show the children how to wind a sticky note round their straw, winding from the edge opposite the glue. Press the glue down to make a tube and slide the tube off the straw.

6. Flatten one end of the straw, so it makes an L shape. Then, put the tube back on the straw. You now have a rocket! Hold the straw, not the sticky note, and blow hard to fire the rocket. Practice!

7. Draw a line with chalk on the ground or the carpet. Line up and see how far you can blow your rocket.

8. Take some photos and talk about why you think this experiment works.

9. Now draw some more lines and have a rocket blowing competition.

Fingers hands and feet

Investigate lines and pattern

What you need:

- A camera
- A clipboard
- At least two adults
- A stamp pad
- Shallow trays lined with thin sponge
- One colour of thick, dark paint (blue, black, red, or brown), just enough to wet the sponge
- Towels and a bucket or bowl of soapy water
- A4 or similar paper for each child
- A roll of lining paper or display paper (white is best)
- Magnifying glasses (optional)

What to do:

1. Help the children to collect all the things you need. Appoint a photographer – but make sure they also have turn at the activity.

2. Explain that you are going to investigate your hands and feet – the children will love it if you get involved too!

3. Firstly, look at your own hands. Magnifying glasses are useful, but the children will be able to see the lines without them.

4. Talk about what you can see. *Are there lines on your hands? Is the back of your hand different from the front? Can you see little hairs on the back of your hand? Do we have hairs on our palms? Can you see the little lines on the ends of your fingers? What do you think they are for?*

5. Give each child a piece of white paper and pass round the stamp pad so they can carefully press the ends of some of their finger on the pad and make a print on the paper. Don't press too hard. Look at the prints. *Are your fingers all the same?*

6. Now take off your shoes and socks and have a look at the soles of your feet. This may be easier for children than adults! *Are there lines on your feet too? What are these for? We don't pick things up with our feet. Do we have little lines on the ends of our toes, like we do on our fingers?*

7. Help the children to make prints of their own feet on some of the paper roll, by pressing gently on a painty sponge and then stepping on the paper. Just do one print of each foot, this is a science activity, not messy play! Write the name of each child beside their prints.

8. Use the bowl of water for washing painty feet.

9. When everyone has done their prints (not forgetting the photographer and any adults), compare the prints of different people. Look at the different lengths, toes, insteps, patterns of lines.

Top tip ⭐

Get lining paper from DIY shops, and use a cheap bath sponge sliced horizontally into thin slices for foot printing.

Taking it forward

■ Use your footprints for measuring activities. Cut them out and write your name on each one. Now use them to measure things in your setting: the carpet, the patio, other children. These are not standard measures, but they are important for developing the concept of measuring.

What's in it for the children?

Scientific processes: Features of living thing, similarities and differences.

Fascinating fact: Scientists think the bigger lines on our palms help us to bend and flex our hands, and all the lines help with feeling and gripping things.

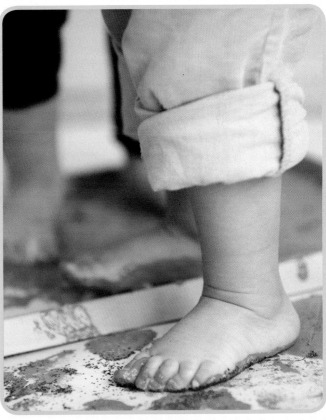

Health & Safety

This is best done outside, and bare feet can slip, so take care.

Give it a grow!
Investigate seeds

What you need:

- A camera
- A clipboard
- Seeds of all sorts and sizes – the best thing to do is to go on an autumn walk and collect your own seeds: acorns, conkers, sycamore 'helicopters', thistle and dandelion heads, beech nuts etc.
- If you can't go on a walk, use one of these: mixed bird seed from a pet shop; dried seeds from a supermarket (lentils, dried peas or beans, rice etc); or ask parents and friends for unused packets of garden seeds
- Magnifying glasses
- A packet of mustard and cress seeds (these are to grow)
- A tray, shallow box or clean plastic food containers
- Kitchen roll or thin sponge sheets, or an old flannel
- Water in a plastic jug or bottle

Top tip

Try to get seeds of varying sizes, shapes and colours.

Health & Safety

The dry seeds don't taste very nice, but warn the children not to eat them.

What to do:

1. Help the children to collect all the things you need. Appoint a photographer.

2. Pour the seeds onto the tray and look at them together. Use magnifying glasses to look at the different parts of the seeds. Can the children see: *Where the seed joined onto the seedpod? How it joined onto the plant or tree? What sort of seed it is?* Talk about what each seed will grow into.

3. Sort the seeds by colour, by size, by what it will grow into (tree/plant), by way of travelling (flying/dropping/sticking onto animals).

4. Carefully break some of the seeds apart: *What is inside? How many bits are there? What will each bit become? What does a seed need to help it grow into a plant or tree?*

5. Collect up these seeds and show the children the mustard and cress seed packet. Look at the differences between the seeds of mustard and those of cress: mustard seeds are round, much bigger than cress, and a lighter colour, cress seeds are small and brown. Read the instructions on the packet for growing them.

6. Help the children to spread some kitchen roll or paper towels on the bottom of a tray or other container. Sprinkle this 'soil' with water, then let the children sprinkle the two sorts of seeds in two halves of the container.

7. Ask the children what the seeds need now.

8. Put the seed trays somewhere warm and light and watch every day to see what happens. Don't forget to water them. When your mustard and cress has grown, make some sandwiches.

Taking it forward

- Cut the bottoms off small plastic water bottles to make little greenhouses. Use the base to plant the seeds, and the top to cover them and keep them warm. Try growing runner beans, orange or apple pips, sunflower seeds, grass seed, melon seeds or chickpeas. Transplant the little seedlings when they get too big for the bottle.

What's in it for the children?

Scientific processes: Living things (plants), sorting, classifying.

Fascinating fact: Most seeds need to be very cold before they can start growing.

Blooming marvels!

What you need:

- A camera
- A clipboard
- Small flowers such as daisies, dandelions, buttercups, and their leaves from your garden, the field or the park
- Small paper or plastic plates
- Magnifying glasses, plastic tweezers
- Paper and a range of drawing tools, thin felt pens, coloured pencils, pastels or chalks

Top tip

Ask your local park keepers if you can come and pick daisies.

aking it forward

- Make observational drawings of plants, flowers and other objects a regular feature of your work, encouraging children to look carefully and record what they see.

Vhat's in it for the children?

cientific processes: Living things plants), naming plant parts

ascinating fact: Some plants don't ave any flowers at all, and some don't ave any leaves

Health & Safety

Flowers should not be eaten, however tempting they look!

What to do:

1. Help the children to collect all the things you need. Appoint a photographer. Sit in a circle on the carpet, or better still outside, either round a table or on a rug on the grass.

2. During the activity, encourage the children to use the correct words for the main parts of the flowers – stem or stalk, petal, leaf and sepal (the green part under the petals).

3. Start by looking at the flowers the children have collected. Give everyone a plate. Take one flower each, and find its matching leaf. Put these on your own plate.

4. Make sure the children know the name of the flower they are looking at – even if they all have the same flower, it's a good idea to go round, each saying the name.

5. Hold the flower by its stalk or stem. Look at the flower carefully, talking about what you see, and using colours, textures, patterns and plant words. The children can use magnifying glasses if you have enough for one each.

6. Look at the petals, carefully describing the colours you see – a daisy petal is not just white! A dandelion petal is not just yellow!

7. Look at the other flower parts – the sepals, the stalk, the leaves and any buds. Encourage the children to name what they can see, showing each other features such as the hairs on a daisy stem, or the veins on the leaves.

8. Now let the children watch as you carefully dissect a flower, using tweezers and careful fingers, and lay the petals, sepals, stamens and leaves out on a plate so the children can see how the flower parts fit together. Take photos at this stage too.

9. Give each child some paper and a choice of drawing tools to make drawings of the flowers they have examined, trying to capture the details of their observations.

It's raining on me!

Investigate waterproofing

What you need:

- A camera
- A clipboard
- Plastic sheets, shower curtains or plastic tablecloths
- Fabric sheets or curtains
- Water in small watering cans or plastic bottles
- Masking tape, sticky tape, and duct tape
- String, clips, pegs and cable ties
- Canes or thin poles, mallets

Top tip

Get cheap plastic sheets and duct tape from 'pound' shops. Ask parents to donate old curtains.

Taking it forward

- Test ways to make fabrics waterproof, by coating them with paint, diluted white glue, or strips of tape.

What's in it for the children?

Scientific processes: Materials, structures.

Fascinating fact: Coating fabric with dilute white glue or school glue will make it water resistant, but not completely waterproof.

Health & Safety

Take care when using plastic sheeting, so children do not get wound up or covered with them.

What to do:

1. Help the children to collect all the things you need. Appoint a photographer, and get ready to do some filming – video clips will help when you are talking about the exploration later.

2. This investigation is good for autumn or spring times when there are frequent showers, and is easier done out of doors.

3. Tell the children you are going to find out what to use to make a den waterproof.

4. Look at all the fabrics and fastenings you have collected. Feel them and discuss which ones would make the most waterproof covering for a den. *How could you test them?*

5. Now use watering cans or water bottles to test the different fabrics and other materials. Hold each fabric up off the ground by its corners, and gently pour water onto it. Look underneath and see if the water comes through. Test each fabric in turn, and put them in two piles – 'waterproof' and 'not waterproof', 'leaky', or any other description the children suggest.

6. When you have decided which is the best, look at the tapes: *Which one do you think will be best to stick the fabric in the rain?* Ask the children how to test the tapes. Use their ideas even if you haven't thought of them yourself. One way would be to dip lengths of the tape in water and then see if the wet tape will stick. Another way would be to stick lengths of tapes on a piece of wood and pour or brush water on them. Leave for a while, then see if they come off.

7. Now build your waterproof den. Help the children to hammer in sticks or canes and use cable ties or string and make their waterproof den. Only help if they ask – if you can't stop yourself, then take the photos to keep yourself busy!

8. When the den is finished, leave the children to play in it. Watch every day to see how waterproof it is. Talk about your experiment together.

A fishy business

nvestigate magnets

What you need:

- A camera
- A clipboard
- Magnets – several different sizes and types if possible.
- Scissors, string
- Paper or card fish shapes for the game
- Paper clips, sticky tape.
- Three or four short garden sticks or chopsticks
- A shallow box, builder's tray or even a dry paddling pool

Top tip

Cut out the fish shapes before the activity to keep the focus on science, not craft!

king it forward

Take your magnets outside and see how many things you can find that are magnetic. Try drainpipes, bricks, stones, manhole covers, door handles, lamp-posts.

hat's in it for the children?

cientific processes: Forces – agnetism.

scinating fact: You can make another agnet by stroking your magnet along ong nail, head to point, over and er again. This will turn the nail into a agnet.

Health & Safety

Store and use magnets carefully. Don't out them near electrical equipment, computers, DVD players or televisions.

What to do:

1. Help the children to collect all the things you need. Appoint a photographer, and get ready to do some filming.

2. Look at the magnets together, and let the children look at them and handle them. *Do you know what magnets can do? Will the magnets stick to your hands? Will the magnets stick together?*

3. Talk to the children about investigating the magnets to find out what they do. Let the children choose a partner to work with, and together, find an object that they think the magnets will pick up and an object they think the magnets won't pick up.

4. Come back to the circle and ask the children to hold up the object they think the magnet will stick to. When they've made their predictions let them try. *What can you see about the things the magnet will stick to or attract?*

5. Tell the children that you're going to make a special fish jumping game with the magnets, but first you need some fish. Show them the fish you have cut out, and help them to fix a paper clip to the nose of each one. *Why are you using a paper clip? What else could you use? What is special about a paper clip?*

6. Cut the string into lengths and tie each to one of the canes/sticks. Tie a magnet on the other end of the string – horseshoe magnets work best for fishing games.

7. Tell the children that the aim is to get the fish to jump up to the magnets, without touching them with the magnet. Put the fish in their 'pond' and take turns to play the game. Make sure the children understand that the magnets should just dangle over the fish without touching them.

8. When everyone has had a turn, write some numbers on the fish and the children can play in pairs. One child calls out a number and the other has to 'catch' that fish – remember the aim is to get the fish to jump up to the magnet, not to dab it.

9. Why do the magnets make the fish 'jump'?

Bend it, shape it

Investigate squashing and stretching

What you need:

- A camera
- A clipboard
- A collection of things that will squash, bend and/or stretch, and some that won't: a piece of elastic, a piece of string, a sponge, a straw, a plastic ruler, a balloon, a rubber ball, a plum, a lump of modelling clay, sticky tac, a newspaper, a tomato, a wooden brick, a rubber, a spring, an elastic band ball, etc.
- Hoops or skipping ropes.
- Coloured stickers or tape (two colours)

Top tip ⭐

Experimenting will destroy some squashy things (such as a tomato) so have some more as backup.

What to do:

1. Collect all the things you need and appoint a photographer.

2. Introduce your collection of bendy, stretchy and squashy things. Talk with the children about what they are, but at this stage, not what they'll do. Let the children play, investigating them and experimenting with them.

3. Ask the children for their comments on the behaviour of the objects they've been handling. Ask them: *Can you squeeze or stretch some objects? When you let go, do they go back to their old shape? Are some things not stretchy? Do some things break or get damaged when you squash or stretch them?*

4. Put three hoops on the floor, or make three circles with skipping ropes. Label one circle 'squashy', one 'stretchy, and one 'not squashy or stretchy'. Ask the children to put the objects in the appropriate circles. When they've done this discuss with them the choices they made. *How did you decide? Are there some things that are both squashy and stretchy? Where did you put them? Why? Could you overlap the circles so an object can be in both circles?*

5. Talk about things that do and don't go back to their original shape after you have squashed or stretched them. *What happens to a piece of elastic? A tomato? A balloon? Are there some things that lose their squashiness or stretchiness by being used over and over again?*

6. *Are people squashy and stretchy? Try stretching parts of your body, which bits stretch, which bits don't? Try gently squashing bits of your body, which bits can you squash? Warn them to do this gently – they are not tomatoes!*

50 fantastic ideas for investigatio

Collect pictures of objects and play a solid/stretchy/squashy game. A caller goes through the pictures, shouting out what they think each one is, and the other children shout 'squashy', 'stretchy' or 'not' according to what they think is appropriate. Talk about any disagreements.

What's in it for the children?

Scientific processes: Materials, forces, changes.

Fascinating fact: Elastic materials and objects will stretch and squash, but will return to their original shape.

Everyone different
Investigate skin

What you need:

- A camera
- A clipboard
- Safety mirrors – A4 size
- Magnifying glasses
- Paper
- Paint palettes or plastic plates and small brushes
- Paint to make skin colours: pink, white, brown, yellow, black, red and purple will all help with the mixing

Top tip

Very young children often don't realise what colour their skin is, be careful and tactful.

Taking it forward

- Make a 'Guess who my friend is' display of the paintings with flaps covering the names, so everyone can guess.

What's in it for the children?

Scientific processes: Living things (humans), similarities and differences.

Fascinating fact: *Skin is there to keep our organs in, and to keep harmful things out.*

Health & Safety

Some children hate having their skin touched – be sensitive.

What to do:

1. Collect all the things you need and appoint a photographer.

2. Pair the children so that each one has a 'talking partner'. Ask them to sit facing their partner, so they can look at and talk about each other's skin. Explain that you are going to do another exploration of themselves and their friends, and start something like this:

3. First you are going to look at the skin on your hands. *Why do we have skin? What does it do? Does it get bigger as you grow? Why does it go wrinkly in the bath?*

4. *What colour is your skin? Is it the same colour on the back of your hand as the palm? Is it the same colour as your partners? Can you see little lines and hairs all over your arms?*

5. Now look at the skin on your legs. *Have you got hairs on your legs? Who has the hairiest legs? Why is the skin on your knees wrinkly?* Feel the skin on your knees, then feel the skin at the back of your knees. *Is it different? What does it feel like?*

6. Look at your friend's face. *What colour is the skin on their face?* Use a mirror to look at both your faces together. *What is the same? What is different about the skin on your two faces?*

7. The next challenge is to mix some skin coloured paint, so that each child can paint a picture of their friend's face. Help them if they need it, and use mirrors, or a tiny dab of paint on their friend's hand to check the match.

8. The pairs of children can work on both paintings together. They will probably need some help, so it's a good idea to have more than one adult available.

Glass in motion
investigate a bag of marbles

What you need:

- A camera
- A clipboard
- Marbles, as many different sizes and kinds as you can collect – plain and coloured glass, stripes, swirls, steel
- A large plastic tray
- Plastic bowls or other containers
- Chalk
- Cardboard tubes
- Cardboard box

Top tip

Marbles you buy from suppliers tend to be all the same size. You'll get a greater variety if you appeal to families for marbles, or look at markets, car boot sales, or charity shops.

Taking it forward

- Use boxes and other recycled materials to make a marble run.

What's in it for the children?

Scientific processes: Forces.

Fascinating fact: Marbles are made from sand, heated in a furnace to make glass, which is made into a rod, coloured, then snipped into bits. These are rolled down a slope while they are still very hot. The rolling makes them into a ball or sphere.

➕ **Health & Safety**

Take care with small marbles, children are very tempted to put them in their mouths.

What to do:

1. Collect all the things you need and appoint a photographer.

2. Tip out the marbles on to the tray and let the children play with them, rolling, swirling and bouncing.

3. Sort the marbles, grouping by size, colour, or what they're made from.

4. *How are marbles made? How do they make them round? How do they get the patterns inside?*

5. Drop marbles one at a time on to the tray. See which bounce, and how far they bounce. *Do glass marbles bounce higher than metal ones? Do big ones bounce higher than small ones?*

6. Draw a circle roughly 15 cm across on the floor. Put five marbles in the middle of the circle. Get the children to choose a marble each from the rest.

7. The children take turns to roll their marbles at the ones in the circle, trying to knock them out of the circle. Watch and talk about what happens when a marble is hit. Return any that are knocked right out of the centre circle. *How do the marbles behave when they're hit? Does the size make a difference? Do glass marbles behave differently?*

8. Make a target by cutting some arches into a cardboard box. Write a scoring number over each arch. Roll the marbles from a chalk line and see what score you can get with two marbles each. Now try rolling the marbles through the cardboard tubes to see if you can use the tubes to aim the marbles at a number your friend chooses.

Making Light of it

Investigate shadows

What you need:

- A camera
- A clipboard
- Large cardboard box
- Thin white paper
- Scissors
- Glue stick
- Small world figures
- Sticky tack
- A torch (the more powerful the better)

Top tip ⭐

If you have somewhere to store it keep the light stage - it's useful for a lot of other activities.

Taking it forward

- Go outside on a sunny day and play games with shadows. Try to do this in the morning and again in the afternoon, and talk about how the shadows are different and why this could be.

What's in it for the children?

Scientific processes: Light.

Fascinating fact: Shadows don't only appear when you stand in the sun, you can get a 'moon shadow' in moonlight

 Health & Safety

Teach the children not to shine lights in people's eyes.

What to do:

1. Collect all the things you need and appoint a photographer.

2. Help the children to make a simple 'light stage' by cutting the lid off a large cardboard box, pasting the inside of the box and lining it with paper.

3. Place the box on its side so that the open end is toward you (like a theatre). Stand one of the plastic figures in the centre of the 'stage'. Get one of the children to stand a metre away from the box, holding the torch very still and level with the figure. Shine the torch beam on the figure and look at the shadow on the back wall.

4. Talk about the shadow. *Why is it there? What happens when you move the torch from side to side? Why does the shadow move?* Keep the torch in the same place at the front and add a couple more figures, one nearer the front of the box and the other closer to the back. Use the sticky tack to keep them in place. *Are the shadows all the same size? Why not?* Move the torch further away and then closer, and watch what happens to the shadows.

5. Add some more characters and make up a story.

6. If you have other suitable models include those too (vehicles, dinosaurs, farm and jungle animals, birds). Let the children decide what their story will be. Maybe they want to bring in their own character figures from films and TV programmes – Doctor Who, Frozen, Superman etc.

7. Take lots of photos as the children create and sequence the story.

8. Use the photos of the exploration to make a PowerPoint presentation or a show for your whiteboard. Show the story and talk about it with the children. They may want to change the order. As they go through the story make some notes and write a simple story to show with the photos.

Keep it cool

investigate a bag of ice cubes

What you need:

- A camera
- A clipboard
- A bag of ice cubes
- Shallow tray or washing-up bowl
- Two plastic bowls or basins
- Hot (not scalding) and cold water
- Clear plastic cups
- A selection of insulators: tinfoil, newspaper, socks or gloves, cotton wool, sweatshirt, cardboard, cling film, plastic bag
- Access to a freezer

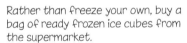

Top tip ⭐

Rather than freeze your own, buy a bag of ready frozen ice cubes from the supermarket.

Taking it forward

- Take some cups of ice outside on a sunny day, ask the children to predict where the ice will melt quickest and where it will last longest and test their predictions.

What's in it for the children?

Scientific processes: Changes, melting.

Fascinating fact: You can build structures from ice cubes, the melting water on the outside of the cube freezes again when it touches another cube.

➕ Health & Safety

No special issues, although make sure hands and fingers don't get too cold playing with the ice.

What to do:

1. Collect all the things you need and appoint a photographer.

2. Tip some ice cubes into a tray and give the children time to investigate them, stirring, rubbing, stacking. Put the rest of the cubes in the freezer.

3. After a time there will be water in the tray. Ask the children: *Where has it come from? Why does ice melt?*

4. Provide two bowls of water: one very warm (but not scalding), the other very cold. Get the children to make observations about the water, testing it with their fingers. *What will happen if you put an ice cube in each bowl. Which cube will melt first? Why?*

5. Carry out the experiment. Watch the ice cubes closely and talk about what's happening. *Was your prediction right?*

6. Take two bowls and put a few (two or three) ice cubes in one and a lot (12–15) in the other. Put one ice cube in each of the two plastic cups and stand one cup in the bowl with a few cubes and the other in the bowl with a lot. *Which cubes do you think will melt fastest?* Observe what happens. *Were you right? Can you think why?*

7. *How could we stop the ice melting?* They may say put it in the freezer but ask for other ideas too. Show the insulators you've provided and ask which they think will work best, which worst.

8. Try some of them out by putting five ice cubes in a plastic cup for each. Space the cups out on the same shelf and cover each with the insulator you're going to try. Watch what happens and decide which preserves the ice longest.

9. Make a display of your experiments, using the photographs your photographer has taken.

Put it in, get it out

Investigate mud

What you need:

- A camera
- A clipboard
- **Some garden soil in a small bowl or bucket** (you need garden soil, not compost from a garden centre for this experiment)
- **Two large empty plastic drinks bottles with screw tops**
- Water in a plastic jug
- A funnel, spoons, plastic tweezers, magnifying glasses
- Plastic gloves
- Coffee filters or paper towels
- Some white plastic plates

Top tip

Ask a gardener to let you have some soil from their garden, it's likely to have more interesting things in it!

What to do:

1. Help the children to collect all the things you need. Appoint a photographer, and give them some gloves too

2. Ask why you all need to wear gloves for this exploration If you can find a picture of scientists working with gloves on, show this to the children.

3. Pass the plates round, and explain that you are going to look at soil or mud. Ask one of the children to carefully spoon a small amount of soil onto each plate, so the children can examine it with their fingers. Talk about how it looks, feels, smells (no tasting!). Encourage and praise describing words – gritty, sticky, crumbly, scratchy.

4. There may be some living things to look at (worms, ants little flies and beetles) look at these too, and name the ones you know. Take them outside and release them.

5. Ask the children what you think will happen if the soil gets very wet. How could you do this with the things you have collected. They will probably suggest using a funnel in one big bottle, so help them to spoon some of the soil into the funnel. If it's a bit lumpy, you may need to poke through with a spoon.

6. Now pour some water through the funnel into the bottle until it is about half full.

7. Put the top on and shake the bottle to mix the soil and water, then put the bottle on a flat surface. Watch what happens. Gradually the soil will sink to the bottom. If you look carefully you will see it falls in layers. Talk about why this must be. (The heaviest particles will fall first, leaving the smallest particles in the water at the top, or even on the surface).

8. Ask the children if they can think of a way to get the soil out of the water again. Take all their suggestions seriously, and try some.

9. If they can't think of a way, suggest using a coffee filter paper inside the funnel. Put this in the neck of the second bottle and gently pour the mud and water mixture through. Watch what happens. *What is left in the filter? Why is the water still brown? Why does some of the mud stay in the water?* (The smallest particles can go through the filter and back into the water).

Taking it forward

Make some more bubble blowers from:

- Draw circles or patterns on coffee filters with water-based felt pens. Fold the filters into quarters, and balance them on glasses of water so the point of the filter just touches the surface of the water. The water will seep up the filter and make wonderful patterns as it reaches the felt pen marks.

What's in it for the children?

Scientific processes: Mixing and separating.

Fascinating fact: The word mud describes a sticky mixture of soil and water. Soil is dry earth.

✚ Health & Safety

Avoid areas that may have been used by animals, and make sure children wash their hands after this exploration, even if they have been wearing gloves.

Fly away

Investigate feathers

What you need:

- A camera
- A clipboard
- Feathers of as many different sizes and kinds as you can find
- Magnifying glasses
- Plastic droppers and pipettes
- A bowl of water
- Paper and drawing tools: felt pens, coloured pencils, crayons in a restricted range of feather colours – browns, greys, oranges, yellows, black

Top tip

If you buy packs of feathers, look online for natural ones, not ones that have been dyed in artificial colours.

Taking it forward

- Go to the school or local library, or on the internet, and look for some books abut birds and feathers. Take your feathers and find out which birds they came from.

What's in it for the children?

Scientific processes: Living things, birds.

Fascinating fact: The hooks on feathers help the bird to fly, by holding the feather together so it resists the air.

✚ Health & Safety

If you want to use feathers that you have picked up on walks, wash them carefully in soapy water and put them in the freezer for a few days to remove any germs or bugs.

What to do:

1. Help the children to collect all the things you need. Appoint a photographer, or one for the exploration and another to record the follow up artwork.

2. Put all the feathers in the middle of the floor or table.

3. Choose a feather each to look at, and talk about. Look at the shaft – the central 'stalk'.

4. Gently push the feather so the little bits at the sides of the shaft (called the barbs) come apart. Show them how you can gently stroke the barbs so they stick back together again. *Why does that happen?* Look with magnifying glasses to see the little hooks that hold the barbs together –very young children may need some help.

5. Ask the children how birds keep dry and even fly in the rain. Try dropping a drop of water onto your feather, and watching what happens. *Does the water soak in or run off? Is the feather waterproof?*

6. Now describe your own feather to a 'talking partner', and listen to them describe theirs.

7. Talk as a group about the colours in the feathers – look carefully. Get your clipboard and make a list of all the colours the children can see and name. You could talk about dark brown or light brown etc.

8. Now put the paper and drawing tools in the centre of the group so each child can draw their own feather. Younger children, and those with less experience of close observation may find this challenging. Praise the efforts of all the children.

9. Make sure you get some photos of the children working as well as their finished drawings.

Come fly with me

Investigate air, wind and flight

What you need:

- A camera
- A clipboard
- A windy day!
- A number of items of various weights and sizes to let loose in the wind, some that will 'fly' and others that won't: feathers, leaves, paper, carrier bag (paper and plastic), polystyrene tile, wooden brick, a magazine, a sock, a tissue, a cloth or duster, balloons (inflated and not)
- Small plastic carrier bags
- Thread or lightweight string

Top tip

You need plenty of space. Make sure that the things that you let blow in the wind can be collected up again.

Taking it forward

- Make a collection of pictures of anything that flies, and of things flying. Divide them into natural and manmade objects. Add them to your display.

What's in it for the children?

Scientific processes: Materials, forces.

Fascinating fact: A glider flies like a kite, it needs something (usually a tractor) to pull it so it gets into the air, then the tractor lets go of the 'string'. Plastic carriers fly the same way – you are the tractor!

Health & Safety

Take care that things don't get blown into eyes.

What to do:

1. Collect all the things you need and appoint a photographer.

2. Go outside on a windy day with the items you've gathered. Feel the force of the wind on faces, arms, bodies. Stand facing the wind and with your backs to the wind and talk about how it feels different. Observe the effects of the wind and talk about them – smoke, trees, clouds, bird flight.

3. Arrange the children in pairs and look at some of the items you have collected. *Which ones do you think will fly in the wind and which won't?* Get each pair to stand a few metres apart, one upwind and one down. The upwind child holds an item in the air and lets go, to see whether it will fly to their partner. Photograph the experiments

4. Talk about their predictions and the results of the experiments. *Were your predictions right? What are the things that make something fly in the wind? What stops things flying? A sheet of paper flies but a magazine doesn't – why is that? Why does a balloon that's blown up fly but not one that isn't?*

5. Talk about other things that fly (birds, insects, planes, rockets, hot air balloons, kites, arrows).

6. Show the children how to make a simple kite by tying the handles of a plastic carrier bag together with a length of string. Help the children make some kites and fly them by running fast with the string behind them.

7. Take some photos. When you come back inside draw some pictures and use these and the photos to make a display.

Where did it go?

Investigate a puddle

What you need:

- A camera
- A clipboard
- A day when it has been raining and the rain has stopped, but there are still puddles
- A meter ruler or tape measure
- Playground chalk
- A sand timer (five minutes) or a kitchen timer with a 'pinger'

Top tip

In rainy weather, note the places where puddles gather, then you will be ready to do this exploration.

Taking it forward

- Make your photos into a slide sequence on PowerPoint, or a flick book so you can see the puddle disappearing.

What's in it for the children?

Scientific processes: Changes, evaporation.

Fascinating fact: The sun makes the air warmer, and it rises back up into the air, taking the water with it through evaporation. The water turns into clouds, and comes down again in the next shower.

What to do:

1. Help the children to collect all the things you need. Appoint a photographer or one for the exploration and another to record the measurements.

2. Say to the children that you need to find a puddle to investigate, so they should not splash or jump in puddles until you have chosen which one to investigate

3. Go outside and look for the biggest puddle you have in your outdoor area.

4. Talk about the puddle and ask the children how they think you could find out how big it is. They may want to use a ruler or a tape measure – or even stand in the middle to see how far it comes up their boots! Choose which method to use and measure the depth of the puddle in the middle. Write this down on your clipboard and take a photo.

5. Now ask the children: *Where does the rain go after a storm or shower. Will the puddle stay like this forever? Where does the water go?*

6. How can you find out if the water in the puddle is getting less – evaporating? Suggest that they could draw round the puddle with the chalk, and come back in a while and see if it is smaller.

7. Use the chalk to draw round the edge of the puddle. You may need to protect your puddle from other groups when they come out. How could you do this? Use a row of chairs, cones, a ribbon or tape , or even a 'police person' from your group.

8. Go inside and set the timer for five or ten minutes – the children can choose how long they should wait. Tell a story, do some counting, sing some nursery rhymes.

9. When the timer pings or the sand is through, go out and look again, measure the puddle again. Is the water still touching the chalk line? If not, what has happened? Draw a new line where the water is now.

10. Carry on investigating your puddle until it has completely evaporated.

Let's roll

investigate moving toys

What you need:

- A camera
- A clipboard
- A large space
- Large plastic storage boxes
- Big wooden bricks
- A barrow or trolley

Top tip

This *activity can be done outside, using a hard surface (e.g. patio, playground) and a soft one (e.g. grass, lawn).*

aking it forward

Investigate Lego or similar models, moving them with their wheels fitted and without.

Get some smaller boxes and do the same activity with small sponge balls.

Vhat's in it for the children?

cientific processes: Forces.

ascinating fact: Friction makes things ss 'slippery' and more difficult to move. smooth surface, such as the patio abs has less friction than the grass or arpet.

What to do:

1. Collect all the things you need and appoint a photographer.

2. Group the children in twos, threes or fours and give each group a box and some bricks. Give them time to investigate these and play with them.

3. Get them to try pushing the empty box across different surfaces - the patio, playground, grass or floor. *Which is easiest? Why? Which is hardest? Why?*

4. Put enough bricks in the box to make it much heavier. Try pushing it again. *Is it harder to push?*

5. Ask one of the children to kneel or sit in the box on top of the bricks. Have a go at pushing it now. *Why is the box harder to move when it has things in it?*

6. *What could they do to make it easier still to move the box? Think about how people move heavy things. What do they use?*

7. *Have you got any wheels you could use to move the boxes? Would a bike be a good thing? Why not? What about a barrow? Why would that be better? Get your barrows and other things with wheels and test them to see which is best for carrying heavy things.*

8. Talk about what you've discovered, and how wheels can be used to move heavier objects more easily.

Health & Safety

Watch out for pinched fingers.

Mixing scientists
Investigate mixing

What you need:

- A camera
- A clipboard
- Five clear water bottles
- Water in a plastic jug; funnel
- Vegetable oil
- Powder paint: red, blue, yellow
- Food colouring: red, blue, yellow
- Duct tape or superglue
- Glitter, sequins or little beads

What to do:

1. Help the children to collect all the things you need. It isn't necessary for every child to have their own bottle (although they would love it) they just need to be able to see what is happening. Appoint a photographer and check that they know what to do.

2. Look at the bottle of oil. Pass it round and let the children tip it around to see how the oil moves. Look through it to see the colour.

3. Now suggest that you are going to be mixing scientists by making the oil different colours, and by mixing some of it with water.

4. Pour some oil into small bowls, and add some powder colour to each. Mix it in with spoons.

5. Help the children to fill each of the empty bottles half full with water, using the jug and funnel. Add food colouring so you have equal numbers of red, yellow and blue bottles.

6. *Which colour of oil do you want to add, and to which bottle? What do you think will happen?*

7. Help to pour the oil into one of the bottles, using the funnel.

8. Fill the bottle almost full. Fix the top on firmly. Shake the bottle and watch what happens.

9. Continue with the other bottles, one at a time, choosing colour mixtures, watching and discussing. Encourage the use of descriptive words: mix, dilute, dissolve, same, different.

10. Add some glitter, sequins or little beads to some of the bottles. Seal the tops on all your bottles with duct tape or superglue (adult only!), and leave the bottles out for the children to play with independently.

Top tip ⭐

Try to get some bottles with smooth surfaces, they make observation much easier.

50 fantastic ideas for investigations

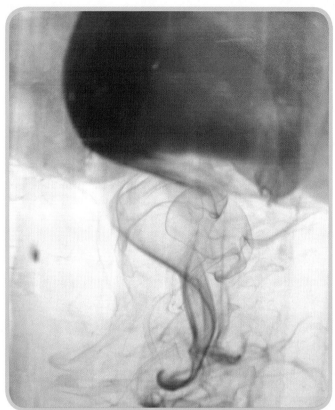

aking it forward

Make another bottle with water and food colouring, and plain oil. Drip a couple of drps of food colouring into the bottle (they should stay on the top of the oil). Then carefully add a very small amount of salt and watch what happens next.

What's in it for the children?

cientific processes: Mixing and eparation.

ascinating fact: At first the oil and water will appear to mix and may even nake a new colour, but as it settles, the il will separate and rise to the top. The il and water will not really mix.

Drink it up
Investigate leaves

What you need:

- A camera
- A clipboard
- **Leaves** (these should be fresh leaves, not fallen ones) **any leaves will do: ivy, dandelion, geranium** – leaves with visible veins will work better
- Scissors
- **Clear plastic cups, glasses or jars**
- Water in a plastic jug
- **Red food colouring** (artificial food colouring works better than the natural sort)
- Magnifying glasses

Top tip

This is a good exploration to do in the spring, when leaves are really young and thirsty.

Taking it forward

- Do the same experiment with some white carnations, so they can see how the food and water needs to travel to the flowers too.

What's in it for the children?

Scientific processes: Living things, plants, nutrition.

Fascinating fact: Gardeners and foresters do pruning in the winter when the trees are dormant and not drinking.

➕ **Health & Safety**

If any children have plant allergies, give them gloves to wear.

What to do:

1. Help the children to collect all the things you need. Appoint a photographer.

2. Explain that you are going to investigate how plants feed their leaves. *How do you think plants drink?* Some may say they drink through their roots, and this is right. The water goes all the way from the roots, up to the leaves and flowers, to feed them.

3. Go into your outdoor area or a park, garden or the woods. You don't need huge numbers of leaves, just a few of each, and choose ones with visible veins or shaft.

4. Back in your setting, look at all the leaves you have collected, and choose one each for your exploration.

5. Cut the end off the stalk or stem of each leaf with the scissors, and help the children to fill a cup or jar about one third full with water.

6. Using a dropper, drop plenty of red food colouring in the cups to make the water really red.

7. Put the leaf in the cup so the stem is in the water, and wait to see what happens. *What do you think will happen?* Some may be able to guess.

8. Wait and watch, and soon you will see the stem of the leaf beginning to show the red colouring. *What's happening now?* Keep watching as the leaf drinks the water, and all the veins become red.

9. Go outside and look at some trees, bushes and plants and talk about the long way water and plant food (minerals) has to travel to get from under the ground to the top of a tree or the end of a branch.

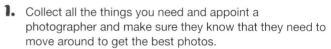

What you need:

- A camera
- A clipboard
- Wooden bricks
- Plastic cups
- A4 thin card
- Small wheeled toys: cars, trucks etc.

Top tip

This works well on an interactive whiteboard.

Taking it forward

Many sports involve pushing a ball, either with the body (football) or using a tool (cricket bat). Find some examples of pushing from sports magazines, books, the internet. *Can you find any sports that involve pulling instead of pushing?* Rowing, tug o' war, weight lifting – which uses both.

What's in it for the children?

Scientific processes: Forces.

Fascinating fact: Some 'pushes' and 'pulls' can't be seen. The wind is a force or 'push' that makes flags fly, turbines spin. It makes clouds move, and plastic bags go up into trees!

What to do:

1. Collect all the things you need and appoint a photographer and make sure they know that they need to move around to get the best photos.

2. Put a toy car on a smooth floor. Ask the children: *Can this car move on its own? Can you move the car without touching it?* Let them try – and someone may blow on it! If they do, explain that the blowing is 'pushing' the car along. *Can you think of some 'pushes' that can move the car by touching it?* Let children try gently with a finger, foot or hand. Explain that these are all 'pushes' that move something that can't move on its own.

3. Mark out a straight course two to three metres long on the floor, with lines at half metre intervals. Choose a vehicle and take turns to send it along the course with a gentle push, and note how far it goes. Then try with a harder push. *Does the toy go further? Why?* Try again with different toys. *Do some toys go further with the same 'push'?* Look closely at the toys. *Can you see a reason why some go further and faster?*

4. Go outside and talk about the equipment there. *Can these toys move on their own? What do they need?* Encourage the children to use the words 'push' and 'pull' in their replies.

5. Firstly, look at trikes, bikes and scooters. *What makes these toys move? Where is the 'push' that makes a trike go? Or a scooter? Or a dolls' pram? What makes a swing go? What makes a football move?*

6. Watch some children demonstrate 'pushes' as they scoot, ride and push the toys. Take some photos.

7. Can the children think of times when the toys need 'pulls' – trolleys, barrows, swings can all be moved by pulling as well as pushing.

Scientific vocabulary

These words may help you in discussions with children – the list is not comprehensive, and many will be to help your own understanding of science, not necessarily for use with the children.

General scientific language: explore, investigate, change, alter, estimate, guess, check, fair test, graph, same, different, separate, change, disappear, measure, weigh, balance, particle.

Hypothesis or theory: a supposition or proposed explanation made on the basis of limited evidence as a starting point for further investigation.

Classify or sort: arrange a group of people or things in classes or categories according to shared qualities or characteristics.

Air and flight: fly, float, land, lift, blow.

Light and mirrors: reflection, shadow, beam, switch, visible, invisible.

Transparent: allowing light to pass through, so that objects behind can be seen clearly.

Translucent: allowing light, but not detailed shapes, to pass through; semi-transparent.

Opaque: does not allow light to pass through at all.

Liquids and solids: liquid, solid, solution, mix, dissolve, wet, dry, evaporate.

Liquid: a substance that flows freely, having a consistency like that of water or oil.

Solid: not liquid or fluid, having three dimensions.

Foam: a mass of small bubbles formed on or in liquid, usually by whisking or shaking.

Steam: the vapour into which water is changed when heated, forming a white mist of minute water droplets in the air.

Surface tension: a property of the surface of a liquid that allows it to resist an external force. It is revealed, for example, in the floating of some objects on the surface of water, even though they are denser than water, and in the ability of some insects (e.g. water striders) to run on the water surface.

Texture: rough, smooth, hard, soft, bumpy, lumpy, gritty.

Heating and cooling: energy, raw, cooked, melt, heat, cool, freeze, melt, dissolve, freeze, frozen.

Waterproofing: waterproof, water resistant, absorbent, dry, leaky, damp, wet, soaking, float, sink, submerged, soluble, insoluble.

Living things: organism (an individual animal, plant, or single-celled life form), living, dead, never lived, decay, mineral, nutrient.

Plants: flower, bud, leaf, sepal, petal, stamen, stalk, root.

Humans: hand, palm, finger, thumb, fingernail, foot, toe, heel, head, face, eye, eyelash, eyebrow, lips, mouth, ear, hair.

Properties of objects and structures: rigid, flexible, inflexible, elastic, bend, stretch, shrink, join.

Structure: a building or other object constructed from several parts.

Forces: move, pull, push, roll, slide.

Net: a pattern that you can cut and fold to make a model of a solid shape or the shape you get when you flatten a box or carton.